Vegetables
from the Sea

Everyday

Cooking with

Sea Greens

Vegetables from the Sea

Jill Gusman

WM
WILLIAM MORROW
An Imprint of HarperCollins*Publishers*

HarperCollins books may be purchased for educational, business, or sales promotional use. For information please write: Special Markets Department, HarperCollins Publishers Inc., 10 East 53rd Street, New York, NY 10022.

FIRST EDITION

Designed by Ralph Fowler

Photographs by Christopher Hirsheimer

Printed on acid-free paper

Library of Congress Cataloging-in-Publication Data has been applied for.
ISBN 0-06-621117-4

02   03   04   05   06   WB/IM   10   9   8   7   6   5   4   3   2   1

For Matthew and Andrea

Contents

Acknowledgments   ix

Introduction   1

How to Use This Book   2

For Time-Conscious Cooks   3

Deep Sea Treasures   3

The History of Sea Vegetables in World Cuisines   9

How Seaweed Is Cultivated and Harvested   11

Sea Vegetables in Your Kitchen   15

Meet the Sea Vegetables   19

Agar   19

Alaria   20

Arame   21

Bullwhip Kelp   22

Dulse   22

Fucus Tips   23

Grapestone   24

Hijiki   24

Irish Moss   25

Kombu   26

Laver   27

Nori   27

Sea Lettuce   28

Sea Palm   29

Wakame   30

Appetizers and Meal Starters   31

Soups and Stews   38

Salads   51

Entrees   67

Side Dishes   83

Rolls, Wraps, and Sandwiches   99

Condiments   108

Sweets and Treats   116

Beauty Secrets from the Sea   123
Mail-Order Sources   124
Index   126

Acknowledgments

Thank you, Adrienne Ingrum, for your enduring vision, dedication, and friendship during the creation of this book and Harriet Bell at HarperCollins for your enthusiasm and commitment to this project from the beginning and for your suggestions along the way to help perfect the manuscript. To Christopher Hirsheimer, our photographer, Kathleen Hackett, our project manager, and to Corrine Trang, our stylist, I extend a special thanks.

It was my time spent at the Kushi Institute with Michio and the late Aveline Kushi, who brought the knowledge of sea vegetables to the West, that I first became aware of sea vegetables. To them and all their teachers, I express my deepest gratitude. Thank you, Annemarie Colbin, for your unique vision for the Natural Gourmet Institute for Food and Health; Diane Carlson, co-director of the Institute, for bringing me into the school and letting me teach public classes on cooking with sea vegetables; and Jenny Matthau, co-director of the school's Chef Training Program, for hiring me to teach many curriculum classes over the years. And, thank you—all my teachers and students. You continue to inspire me.

Thank you, my beautiful children, Matthew and Andrea, for your love and patience and for helping me keep life in perspective, and of course, for your enjoyment of endless seaweed dishes during the making of this book.

Barry, my husband and friend, thank you for believing in me, tasting yet another sea vegetable dish, and relishing the bags of seaweed in our kitchen.

Thank you, Carl Karush, at Maine Coast Sea Vegetables for seaweed. Immense thank yous to Kate Marionchild at Rising Tide Sea Vegetables for inviting me into the world of sea vegetable harvesting and sharing your love of the sea and your wealth of knowledge of these plants. Heartfelt thanks to Larry Knowles at Rising Tide, who patiently guided me through freezing waters with kindness and generosity. To all the harvesters I shared early mornings with and to my family and friends who were a part of the journey from day one, I love you all.

Vegetables
from the Sea

Introduction

Sea vegetables, the "other" seafood, have for centuries held an esteemed place in the cuisine of not only Japan but of Ireland, Scandinavia, precolonial North and South America, Hawaii, Polynesia, Australia, and New Zealand, as well as most nations in Asia, especially Indonesia, the Philippines, China, and Korea. No longer limited to Japanese restaurants, sea vegetables now appear on a wide variety of restaurant menus and in home kitchens everywhere.

I've been cooking with these delicious deep sea treasures for more than twenty years, and I'm delighted to see them, with their great health benefits, becoming more popular. I have shared these delicious deep sea treasures with hundreds of enthusiastic students in my cooking classes and many more appreciative diners whom I've catered and cooked for over the years. Surprise is the almost inevitable response when a sea vegetable is discovered to be the unidentifiable but delicious ingredient in a dish. When revealing the history of edible seaweed and its incredible health benefits, I am often cornered for further questioning, with requests for purchasing information, cooking instructions, and, of course, recipes.

Here is everything you need to know to purchase, store, and cook sea vegetables, with details on individual varieties and interesting information on their history as food, how they are grown and harvested, and why—besides their great taste—it is important to include them in our diets today. With information on recent discoveries about the health benefits of sea vegetables, I've included nutritional facts about these mineral-rich foods.

Recipes are included for every part of the meal. Some are inspired by the wide range of cultures in which seaweed has culinary traditions but has been adapted for Western palates. You'll find basic soups such as Italian Fava Bean and Curried Sweet Potato, as well as Chicken Noodle Stew. There are sandwiches that almost sneak these sea vegetables into well-known favorites. For example, try DLTs, a crowd-pleasing variation of a bacon, lettuce, and tomato sandwich (BLT), where dulse outshines bacon, according to many sea vegetable converts.

There are more adventurous recipes for those who already know and love sea vegetables and are ready for dishes that feature these deep sea treasures front and center. Acutely aware and approving of the growing trend toward health-conscious diets, I have also provided recipes that vegetarians and those cutting down on their red meat intake will enjoy.

I have truly enjoyed seeking out the traditional recipes of other cultures that include seaweed and adapting them for today's taste and cooking styles. Dulse-Filled Irish Soda Muffins, Taiwanese Fishermen's Soup, and many recipes from other Asian countries are my humble efforts to continue the long history of using the sea's vegetation for delicious nourishment.

My approach to serving any new or unusual foods is to prepare them simply in more familiar dishes as one of the ingredients. This way everyone focuses on the dish, not the unfamiliar ingredient.

How to Use This Book

If you already cook with sea vegetables, you'll want to start right in with some of the recipes where they take center stage—Sweet-and-Sour Sea Palm Stew, Crunch 'n' Brine Salad, Baked Sea Vegetable Rolls, or even one of the sea vegetable treats such as Three-Berry Kanten. Seaweed aficionados may want to draw from the book its detailed preparation and culinary treatment of sea vegetables and use my recipes simply as ideas upon which to improvise their own.

Perhaps you've developed a taste for sea vegetables from restaurant dining but have never cooked with them at home. If you have cooked with them, your use may have been limited to nori in sushi and sashimi or adding a strip of wakame to soup pots. For you, full information is provided on the most readily available varieties and everything you need to know to make the other varieties of sea vegetable staples in your pantry and regular cooking ingredients. Start with some of the simpler recipes or those similar to those you've enjoyed in restaurants—Classic Miso Soup, Sea Vegetable Caesar Salad, Sweet-and-Sour Tofu Stir-Fry, Nori-Wrapped Sole, or Hijiki Snow Peas.

If this is your first foray into these fantastic treasures from the sea, you may want to introduce them into your kitchen and to your taste buds gradually. Start with such recipes as Dulse-Filled Irish Soda Muffins, Smoked Dulse and Goat Cheese Salad, Roasted Salmon

Steaks with Kombu, Chicken Stroganoff, Dulse Mashed Potatoes, or Simply String Beans (with a sprinkle of seaweed). Regardless of how familiar you are with edible seaweed, you can introduce it—and its delightful tastes and super nutritional values—into your daily cooking.

For Time-Conscious Cooks

Managing a family with kids and having a career, I understand the importance of getting food on the table with few complications. No one wants to cook for hours after a full day. There are so many concerns throughout the day for everyone; mealtime can be that special time to talk and relax. I have experimented over the years to find ways to keep the preparation and cooking times of my recipes to a minimum. Some sea vegetables require a long cooking time, and when that's the case, I advise you to prepare the recipe in stages—do one step the night before, so when you get home from work the rest of the preparation is a breeze. In general, though, you will find it takes little time to get these tasty recipes on the table.

Food is life, life is passion. For me, being able to put my love for life into my dishes brings me and others I serve great pleasure and satisfaction. Let food be presented with color in a fun, inviting style. Our first bites are with our eyes! The photographs are intended to prove how gorgeous and appetizing these deep sea treasures can be.

May every day be an adventure full of pleasures, surprises, and wonderment while we cook. Relax, have fun, and most important, don't take yourself (or sea vegetables) too seriously. The possibilities are endless and the variations limitless.

Deep Sea Treasures

Edible seaweed, also called sea vegetables, refers to marine growths or algae. For centuries it has proved delicious, highly nutritious, and versatile in cooking. Seaweed grows in polar and tropical seas, usually near coastlines where it attaches to undersea rock formations. Sea vegetables—seaweed that is harvested for eating—are taken only from plants attached to the ocean floor and rocks in deep water. Most edible seaweed is harvested in cold ocean waters. In the United States, harvests take place off the coasts of Maine and Washington, although some of the most delicious wakame, kombu, and sea palm are gathered off the coast of Mendocino, California.

There is great diversity among sea vegetables in appearance, texture, color, and flavor. Some varieties, like nori, are sweeter than others, while others, like hijiki, have a more robust, salty flavor.

Like land vegetation, seaweed contains chlorophyll. Chlorophyll enables it to make its own food through photosynthesis, the same process by which land plants use sunlight to make water and sugar from carbon dioxide. While "weed" is a misnomer for these valuable plants, "vegetable" isn't accurate either, because sea vegetables do not have a root system or flowers. Instead, they attach themselves to rocks, shells, or the sea floor with a rootlike anchor, called a holdfast, that prevents them from being washed away. A frond, which corresponds to a stem or leaf in a land plant, keeps the plant afloat and allows it to drift with the currents. It is the growth on the fronds that is the harvested portion of most edible seaweed. Generally speaking, most growing seaweed is flexible, thin, fairly smooth, and leaflike in shape. It varies greatly in length. Some varieties have small, delicate branches.

The ocean depths, according to many, are less explored by us than space, so it will come as no surprise that, although there are 7,000 recorded seaweed species, we are familiar with just a few. Sea vegetation grows in all oceans and is classified into three ocean zones: warm (tropical and subtropical), temperate, and cold (including subarctic and arctic). The color of the vegetation varies by zone: brown, red, or green. There are almost too many exceptions to state the rule, but in general, brown seaweed, such as kombu, prefers cold water; the red ones grow in tropical and subtropical temperatures. Green varieties grow in all water climates but decrease in abundance as the temperature drops. The smallish seaweed tends to prefer shallower water. The browns, like kelp, can grow to 200 feet with long leaflike extensions on their fronds, while the red varieties, like dulse, tend to be small and feathery.

Temperature has generally opposite effects on sea vegetables and those raised in soil. When the water is warm, plants generally grow slowly and not very large. Seaweed in tropical waters may reach a height of only one to two feet. In cold waters, plants can grow into dense forests of luxuriant seaweed, averaging ten to twelve feet. Cold rather than warm zones produce the largest quantities of edible seaweed.

A Word of Caution

Most of us have at some time been at the beach at low tide when uprooted seaweed drapes the coastline. These plants are never to be picked up for eating, because they are in a state of decay. Their smell is not pleasing, and this seaweed is often sticky and sandy. Regardless of its smell or appearance, once uprooted—or unanchored—seaweed is not edible. *It must not be eaten*. It's fun to examine to see how diverse sea foliage is, but this is not, under any circumstance, seaweed to eat or taste—even if it is dried.

Other factors influence the taste, texture, and quality of sea vegetables, including the seasons where it grows, the tides, and the depths at which the plant lives.

The different seas across the globe all provide unique growing environments for sea plants, and it is amazing how they adapt to a particular environment. For example, wakame from northern Japan is slightly chewier than wakame from California, which is usually quite tender.

All of the recipes in this book use dried seaweed. Sea vegetables are only available dried in most parts of North America and Europe. I've enjoyed the delicious treat of fresh, just-harvested bullwhip kelp, wakame, sea palm, and kombu. Fresh seaweed can sometimes be found in Japanese markets, including those in North America and Europe. But I caution against using any "fresh" sea vegetables unless you have harvested them with an experienced person. This is so important to food safety that I will mention it again and again throughout the book. If you buy fresh sea vegetables, know that they may have developed bacteria during the trip from ocean to grocer. Make sure you know their origin and how they have been handled. Remove any impurities by careful rinsing and preferably by cooking, before you eat them. Drying assures that the seaweed is safe, quality food. The simple process for rehydrating the sea vegetables is included in each recipe.

Extraordinary Food Values

Sea vegetables are among the most nutrient- and mineral-rich foods on the planet. In Japan, seaweed makes up 10 percent of the diet. Some researchers credit sea vegetables in part for the fact that the Japanese experience the lowest incidence in all the industrial nations of some forms of cancer and other illnesses such as heart disease, osteoporosis, and diseases related to obesity.

Sea vegetables have 10 to 20 times more usable minerals than vegetables grown on land. Their health benefits are undisputed. Because they are so rich in minerals, they aid in the growth of nails, hair, bones, and teeth.

Many advocate the addition of sea vegetables to our diets to compensate for lost nutrient value in foods due to denatured soil and overprocessing. If this is your concern, kelp is on the way! Sea vegetables are a positive alternative to the current trend of consuming a daily handful of expensive vitamin and mineral supplements. My preference is to obtain the greatest number of nutrients from the highest-quality whole foods on a daily basis. The body can best use vitamins and minerals in the form in which nature provides them—as food.

The properties of sea vegetables make them seem miraculous in light of today's concerns about healthy eating. Sea vegetables are low in fat but high in dietary fiber. These concentrated food sources are excellent additions to diets that are either lowfat, no fat, or vegetarian.

Good nutrition simply means your diet is balanced by five basic elements: carbohydrates, protein, fats, vitamins, and minerals. Sea vegetables contain all five (see chart).

Nutritional Analysis of Four Sea Vegetables Harvested in the United States

	Kombu (Laminaria dentigera)	Wakame (Alaria marginata)	Dulse (Rhodomenia palmata)	Nori (Porphy perforato)
Protein-gms	7.3	12.7	25.3	35.6
Fat-gms	1.1	1.5	3.2	0.7
Carbohydrates-gms	55	48	44	44.3
Fiber-gms	3	3.6	1.3	4.7
Ash-gms	22	18	22	8
Calcium-mgs	800	1,300	567	260
Potassium-mgs	5,300		8,100	510
Sodium-mgs	3	1.1	2.1	0.6
Magnesium-mgs	760		220	
Phosphorus-mgs	240	260	270	
Iron-mgs	100	13	150	12
Iodine-mgs	150	13	8	
Vit.A-IU	430	140		11,000
Vit.B_1	.08	.11		.25
Vit.B_2	.32	.14		1.24
Vit.B_{12}	50	60		
Niacin-mgs	5.7	10		10
Vit.C-mgs	15	29	49	20

Sources for chart: U.S. Dept. of Agriculture; Japan Nutritionist Association; Composition and Facts About Foods (Ford Heritage Health Research, Mokelumne Hill, CA, 1698); Seaweeds and Their Uses (V. J. Chapman, Methuen & Co. Ltd., London, 1950); "Kelp" (Roseann C. Hirsch, Bestways); "Food from the Sea" (Mary Schooner, East/West Journal, vol. 1, no. 6).

The carbohydrates release slowly, which may stabilize blood sugars. The protein is highly concentrated and provides 25 percent more protein than cow's milk. The fat content is extremely low. The addition to our Western diet of a source of lowfat, no-cholesterol protein makes sea vegetables valuable. Their vitamin supply rivals the best of land plants (for example, dark leafy greens) and are important sources for those hard-to-get B vitamins.

The most important reason to eat these foods from the sea, however, is their mineral content, which is higher than that of any other food category—period.

Calcium maintains bones and teeth and regulates the nervous system. Irritability can be a sign of calcium deficiency. Some varieties of sea vegetables provide 10 times as much calcium as cow's milk, making them an important component in vegan diets.

Iodine is essential for metabolic function. The body needs this mineral as it turns food into energy. Without iodine, our bodies cannot process the carbohydrates, fats, and proteins we eat to maintain our cells and tissues. It also helps regulate the nervous system. A spoonful or two of a sea vegetable provides the recommended daily allowance.

Potassium Seaweed has a high potassium content, making them excellent for nerves, muscles, and the heart.

Iron is the key factor in hemoglobin, which regulates oxygen in the blood. Sea vegetables are high in iron.

Trace minerals Scientists have yet to isolate exactly how the body uses all the various elements essential to good health. However, they have identified "trace minerals" that they know are required. These include magnesium, zinc, and others richly found in sea vegetables.

While researchers are not sure how much of certain minerals and other nutrients we need, it is established that sea vegetables contain a host of other beneficial substances: live enzymes, phytochemicals (used in Asian traditional medicine to treat tumors and bacterial and viral disorders), amino acids, and chromium.

Sea vegetables are said to

Rebalance hormones • Reduce water retention • Decrease bad blood cholesterol levels • Stabilize blood sugars (kombu) • Aid in treating digestive disorders • Cleanse the intestinal tract • Purify and alkalize the blood • Act as an antioxidant • Help metabolize insulin in diabetics • Prevent flatulence • Aid digestion • Cleanse lymphatic system • Enhance immune system

A Special Kind of Sodium

Salt has almost become taboo in some places, and deservedly so, because of the kind and quantity of salt in the average diet. But salt is an essential mineral, a necessary component of body fluids and tissues, and should be used judiciously.

Since they grow in saltwater, you would naturally assume sea vegetables to be loaded with sodium, but that isn't true. The soaking process—part of the preparation for all the recipes in this book—leaches out much of the sodium. Some seaweed contains only moderate amounts of salt. An article in *Natural Health* magazine (September 2000) equates the sodium in a half cup of arame or hijiki to that in a half cup of Raisin Bran—120–160 mg. A serving of dulse has less sodium than a slice of commercially baked bread or a cup of cooked beet greens.

The quality and purity of the sodium in sea vegetables is far superior to that of common table salt. As far as the use of salt is concerned, I suggest buying high-quality sea salt to use daily in cooking for flavor and for strengthening the immune system. Avoid any salt that contains additives, including free-flowing agents.

Food Limitations

Sea vegetables are a good source of minerals for those who may be deficient because of food allergies, such as lactose intolerance, vegetarianism, or those who cook for someone with any of these concerns.

Disease Fighters

Seaweed can play a powerful antitoxic role, helping our bodies fight disease that results from our own toxins as well as those that stem from a polluted environment.

The minerals and enzymes in seaweed aid the body in eliminating toxic elements from the environment and from poor-quality foods, as well as from exposure to radioactivity. A component of seaweed, alginic acid (sodium alginate), acts upon any metallic elements found in the intestines, turning them into insoluble salts, which are then easily eliminated from the body. Without this miracle addition to our cooking, many toxins would remain in the body.

When a family member is having dental work requiring X rays, I always prepare tasty seaweed soup the day before. This ensures a stockpile of minerals waiting to gather radiation and metal residues and move it on!

Besides bringing new flavors to our palates, sea vegetables can improve our health, energy, and vitality. They are excellent sources of protein, are without fat, and are very low in calories. Since all seaweed is high in protein, it can be a staple of your kitchen. Because these foods are concentrated, my rule of thumb is: eat plenty of fresh land vegetables when you eat sea vegetables. And, just because something is good for us does not mean "the more the better." Nature is exquisite about setting limits. With an excess of anything, we can become out of balance. Experiment and learn what works best for you. As for newcomers, small amounts will adjust one's palate to these new tastes. Enjoy and be well!

The History of Sea Vegetables in World Cuisines

From their common pairing with the humble potato as a staple food in Ireland, Norway, and Iceland, to food for royalty in Hawaii, seaweed has been used for centuries as nourishment by seaside cultures the world over. Harvesting local vegetables from the sea was as much a part of life as fishing. Today, culinary tradition continues with the resurgence of seaweed cuisine.

Japan

The Japanese remain the world's number-one consumers of sea vegetables. They enjoy more than twenty varieties and have incorporated them into their cuisine as wraps and garnishes in soups, salads, stir-fries, tempura, and rice dishes, as well as in making jellies. The Japanese alone consume more than 9 billion sheets of nori per year! Other popular varieties include kombu, wakame, arame, and hijiki. They are the largest commercial cultivators and exporters of seaweed. At the same time, they are the greatest importers of harvested wild seaweed.

It is largely the spread of Japanese cuisine to the West that has cultivated our palates for sea vegetables. The popularity of macrobiotic cooking in the 1960s and 1970s gave many Westerners their first bite of these "other" seafoods. Sushi bars, found in major cities across the globe, are single-handedly responsible for introducing the delicious sea vegetable nori.

Many of the recipes in this book are influenced by Japanese cooking, simply because the Japanese have a continuous culinary tradition of using seaweed. The Japanese have discovered the greatest variety of compatible ingredients and perfected preparation and cooking techniques that bring out the flavors of these foods.

Other Asian Cuisines

Koreans, Chinese, Vietnamese, Thai, Burmese, Indonesians, and other Asian people have unique cuisines that include sea vegetables, although none seems to use it quite as extensively as the Japanese.

Korea is a major wakame harvesting nation, and I've adapted for the Western palate a traditional Korean Wakame and Beef Soup (page 50). A popular Thai and Vietnamese pudding-like dessert includes the sea vegetable agar, which is also used in many Asian cuisines for making jellies. See Apple Cider Gel (page 122) for a Yankee rendering.

Ireland and Britain

The people of the British Isles incorporate seaweed into a number of traditional foods and drinks. A favorite Irish milk drink contains dissolved carageenan. A traditional Welsh breakfast delicacy is laverbread, made from laver, the local seaweed (also traditionally served with seafood), rolled with oatmeal and fried into cakes. Dulse is sold and eaten dried as a chewy snack, and traditionally cooked with that most Irish of foods—potatoes (Dulse Mashed Potatoes, page 96).

So Irish is seaweed that the thickening agent carageenan used so frequently in the commercial food industry is named for the Irish village Carragheen, where it was once harvested abundantly. Unlike Japanese culinary traditions, sea vegetables did not survive the transition from the days when foods were grown, hunted, or gathered to today's diet of mostly commercially produced foods, and thus fell out of common use. Fortunately, a few cooks and food folklorists have held on to old kitchen traditions and are bringing back these delicious Irish and Welsh seaweed dishes.

West Indies

Because of seaweed's coagulating qualities, one of the most common uses in all cultures for sea vegetables is the preparation of jellies. While local seaweed is used for that purpose in

Sea vegetables are widely used in the Western food industry today, and you have probably eaten them in a disguised commercial form. Food manufacturers use them to stabilize textures in ice cream, jelly, jam, condensed milk, and soup; to thicken smoothie-type drinks; and as a clarifying agent in manufacturing beer, sake, and wine. Agar seaweed is often incorporated as a filler in canned meats. If you're in the habit of reading labels on the processed foods you buy, you've probably noticed "carageenan," "algin," or "sodium alginate." These are thickening agents that are found exclusively in seaweed—carageenan in red algae and algin in brown algae.

Unfortunately, the dietary and health benefits of the sea vegetables are lost when they are used in these highly processed foods.

In Alaska, seaweed is washed, dried, and rolled for use as chewing tobacco.

the West Indies, a more widely known use is in "sea moss"—male virility tonics. These are generally hot water extracts flavored with a red algae called *gracillaria*, which are made in Jamaica, Trinidad, St. Lucia, Barbados, Belize, and the Virgin Islands.

Native America

It is not surprising, given the bounty of seaweed on both North American coasts, that Native Americans harvested and ate sea vegetables, but, these practices mostly have been lost. Wildcrafter and seaweed researcher John Lewallen learned about Kashaya nori-gathering practices during the 1970s. "Whole clans visit their rocky seashore to gather tender young blades, pulling them from the rocks and drying them in thin mats on nearby tables, sheets, logs or rocks. Sandy blades are rinsed in the sea. It is a joyous, communal time, an ancient earth-bonding in a difficult modern era . . . Aboriginal Natives usually deep-fry the *mei bil* [nori] in fat, making a crisp, tasty, nutritious food enjoyed all year."

How Seaweed Is Cultivated and Harvested

Harvesting

Wild and cultivated seaweed are harvested from oceans and seas around the earth. Major areas of harvest are the Pacific and Atlantic coastlines in the United States, Mexico, and Canada, especially Maine (Maine Coast Sea Vegetable Company), Nova Scotia (Acadian Sea Plants), California (Mendocino Sea Vegetable Company and Rising Tide Sea Vegetables), and Washington (Ryan Drum's Sweetwater Herb Farm), as well as the Japanese and Chinese coasts. Smaller but significant harvests are made in Ireland and Great Britain (Carabay Seaweeds, Galway, Ireland).

Harvesting seaweed by hand is akin to fishing, and harvesters are often referred to as "wildcrafters." The outstanding quality of sea vegetables available in the United States is in large measure due to the experience and respect for nature of wildcrafters. These intrepid outdoorspeople set off by boat or on foot in search of seaweed, often climbing up and down rocky seaside cliffs and poking around in caves when the tide is at its lowest point. Experienced harvesters know where seaweed grows, because it is attached to rocks and generally reappears each year or every few years in the same place—provided it has not been overharvested. In proper harvesting, only the blades (the leaflike growths) are cut. The holdfasts, which attach the plant to the rocks or the ocean floor, and the stipes, its stemlike growths, are not removed. Harvesters wear full wet suits and, from their boats, or standing in shallow water at low tide, or from the edges of seaside cliffs, cut the seaweed using knives. They place the seaweed in large mesh bags to allow for drainage and haul it into their boats or kayaks.

As with any harvest, the key is timing, but when harvesting sea vegetables the tides are critical. At the time of very low tides, called "minus tides," coastal seaweeds are best harvested. Minus tides occur in the few days before and after the new and full moons. Harvesters monitor these especially low tides. At minus tides during abundant growth seasons, they can find the seaweed growing from rocks that are exposed or visible in the very shallow waters.

Most seaweed in the Northern Hemisphere grows rapidly during the cold early spring. On both the Pacific and Atlantic north coasts of North America, late spring is the harvest season for sea vegetables. (The spring harvest starts much later on the east coast than on the west.) Harvest season can last all summer, depending on the locale and variety of sea vegetable.

Once the plants are cut and bagged, they are hauled to shore, then rinsed in fresh water and placed on screens or hung out on lines in the sun to dry.

The widespread use of sea vegetables in Japanese and other Asian cuisines, its use in Western commercial foods and cosmetics preparation, as well as its growing acceptance in diets in the United States, Great Britain, and Europe, has led to large-scale commercial harvesting and drying. Commercial harvesters search out undiscovered wild beds of edible varieties of sea plants, often acquiring leases for coastal harvesting. This is especially true in California and Mexico. Their harvesting methods are sometimes the same as those used by wildcrafters but on a much larger scale. More frequently, commercial harvesters use huge suction machines. The mechanical harvesters do not leave the holdfasts or enough plant material in place for the seaweed to regenerate. Their drying methods differ, also; they usually use dehydration machinery rather than line-drying in direct sunlight. Mechanical drying makes the sea vegetables tougher than natural drying.

Overharvesting and a Solution

Large coastal areas of eastern Canada in the provinces of Nova Scotia and New Brunswick have been vacuumed clean of seaweeds with huge suction harvesters. Conservation groups, as well as the small number of hand-harvesters, are extremely alarmed at the prospect of near-total scouring of Maine coastal seaweeds.

I have seen the results of 20 years of hand-harvesting in some bays of Maine and agree that the [hand] harvest is more than sustainable. I have personally observed similar sustained growth and regrowth in the areas where I have harvested seaweeds for over 30 years.

It is long past overdue for the industries that need to use huge quantities of seaweeds to start investing in off-shore mariculture of fast-growing macroalgae. These seafarms could easily be fabricated and anchored similar to existing Nori farm nets.

—*Ryan Drum, Ph.D., wildcrafter and leading lecturer on sea vegetables*

Each variety of seaweed behaves differently based upon its origin and climatic influences; however, after harvesting, sea vegetables generally deteriorate and discolor faster than land vegetables. In order to preserve any seaweed, you must wash it quickly in fresh water to remove excess sea salt; dry it in steady, direct sun or with commercial drying equipment; and store it in a dark, dry place.

Again, as with fish, wildcrafters generally sell their seaweed to commercial packagers who bring it to the marketplace. The resources list at the back of the book provides contact information for packaged seaweed, as well as wildcrafters who harvest, package, and sell their own seaweed bounty directly.

A Harvesting Experience   Despite two decades of cooking and eating sea vegetables, nothing could have prepared me for my first hands-on sea vegetable harvest. My experience with these incredible plants growing in the sea, alongside rocky cliffs, and near the shoreline, will forever linger in my memory. To witness sea vegetables in their natural habitat has brought me a deeper understanding and appreciation of them. My deepest gratitude to Kate Marionchild and Larry Knowles, who not only took me out on daily harvests in northern California for sea palm, kombu, wakame, nori, and dulse, but shared generously their knowledge, love of the sea, and extraordinary commitment to providing the cleanest, best-quality sea vegetables on the market.

Each harvest is unique, determined by the weather, location, type of seaweed being harvested and, of course, the tide. A typical harvest day begins the night before, when all the equipment is loaded in the trucks. This includes five-gallon buckets with straps, inner tubes with nets, lots of netted bags and sharp knives, a wheelbarrow, and a kayak. I rose at 4:30 A.M. to catch the lowest tide and dressed in full wet suit, including gloves and boots.

Harvesting via deep-sea diving

Another method of hand-harvesting is to dive to depths of twenty to thirty feet to harvest by hand. This method is uncommon but sometimes practiced in warmer climates. It is difficult and tedious and requires expert knowledge of tides and of the edible varieties of seaweed.

Despite the early summer season, those northern California mornings were very cold as was the water temperature. Wearing a wool hat and down parka over my wet suit, I rode in a truck with experienced harvesters to the location of the day's harvest and unloaded equipment in the dark.

The full moon was still visible on the horizon, while behind me was the rising sun. Despite a water temperature in the forties, I walked into the water in search of seaweed. The first moment cold water filled my boots, I wondered if I could survive this adventure. Standing on rocks alongside the pounding waves, holding a bucket and a knife to cut sea palm, I understood that I must never take my eye off the water. This type of harvest can be deadly if a wave sneaks up from behind and lands on you. Bending over to admire the elegance of these plants, however, it is easy to forget the merciless sea around you. I survived that first day, and every day after that, and I felt a kinship with the sea, the amazing plants, and the team of harvesters, who all worked hard within sight of each other.

As taught by the other harvesters, I reached down into the cold water, pulled up long blades, then checked their quality before cutting. We cut only medium-size plants, because they have the best texture and flavor. We did not cut any small blades or any that were too big or tough.

By late morning, as the tide began to roll back in, we loaded our filled sacks into the wheelbarrow for the long haul uphill to the truck. By this time, I was warm, or at least I thought I was. The variations in temperature were incredible.

We loaded everything on the truck. Back at the cottage, we unloaded, and I peeled off the wet suit and put on dry clothes. Some seaweed was brought for a quick rinse and hung out to dry in the sunlight. Others were spread in a thin layer on large screens on long tables and set in the sun to dry. All the plants were carried by hand to the drying house, where they would be protected from the cold, moist night air. The drying house has just enough warm air to finish the drying process gently without causing any dramatic changes to the seaweed. This careful drying and handling ensures a superior quality product.

Cultivation

Cultivated seaweed is started from zoospores—the initial algae cells—placed in saltwater tanks that contain plastic filaments. As they mature, the zoospores develop into juvenile fronds. The plastic filaments are set in a gridlike pattern, and when the fronds are sturdy enough, the grids of fronds are transplanted into the sea. When the plants have reached maturity, the large grids with mature plants attached are pulled up, brought to dry land, and prepared for packaging the same way as wild sea vegetables.

This practice of artificial cultivation has been expanded in Asia to meet the demands of the Japanese diet. Harvested wild seaweed could not have kept up with the demand, and overharvesting would have eliminated many species.

Sea Vegetables in Your Kitchen

Shopping for Sea Vegetables

Sea vegetables are widely available in health food stores, Asian markets, some supermarkets, and gourmet shops. You'll usually find them among the dried packaged foods. Seaweed for culinary use should only be bought dried. Exceptions to this admonition are the small packages or containers of delicious pickled seaweed, eaten as condiments. Sea vegetables are available in prepacked, marinated seaweed salads in some Japanese markets, but these are not used in any of the recipes in this book.

As mentioned before, a huge variety of dried sea vegetables is available. When buying from markets that sell them in bulk, always check the state or country of origin. After a bit

Harvesting is for experts only

With the return of each summer season and trips to the beach, I am reminded of the wealth of vegetation below the surface of the water. In areas with lots of rocks, I often feel seaweed floating around my legs as I swim. These sea plants and pieces lying on the beaches are *not* edible, clean, nutritious sea vegetables. They should not be harvested under any circumstances.

Just as you would not sample the grasses on a nature trail, divers, sailors, motorboaters, and others who may encounter seaweed should *not* harvest seaweed for food. Harvesting seaweed is only for experienced wildcrafters who have expert knowledge of the edible varieties.

of experimentation, you'll learn the differences in taste and texture among the same varieties harvested or cultivated in different parts of the world.

When you shop for seaweed, buy brands from reputable companies that ensure quality control. Among the best sea vegetables are those available from small companies whose experienced wildcrafters harvest, dry, and sell their own seaweed (see Mail-Order Sources, page 124). Purchasing from such companies is akin to buying produce from organic farmers. When buying from these harvesters, you can be sure of getting the purest, highest-quality sea plants and know that the most natural, environmentally safe processes were used in harvesting. Wildcrafters are careful to harvest only where the water remains unpolluted and to cut only the fresh growth of mature sea plants.

A wide variety of good-quality products containing seaweed is available. Tempeh, a fermented soybean product, can be bought with seaweed mixed with the soybeans. This product has a beautiful texture and contrast of light and dark colors. It is a great addition to many dishes for strength and vitality (for example, Hijiki with Deep-Fried Tempeh, page 82). In seitan, or "wheat meat," the liquid in which the pieces of wheat gluten are packaged contains stock made with kombu for depth of flavor. Chips and crackers containing nori, dulse, and kombu can be found in the snack section.

When cooking time is limited, reach for ready-to-shake containers of dried and crushed seaweed in the condiment section of health food stores or other markets. Some include toasted seeds and give a great flavor boost to cooked grains, noodles, and potatoes.

Packets of instant noodles with dried seaweed make flavorful broths.

A favorite of my son's is "kombu candy"—chewy pieces of sweetened kombu that come in an edible potato wrapper. These are special treats that mommies are happy for kids to eat because of their mineral-rich content.

Storing Sea Vegetables

After you purchase sea vegetables, store them unopened in their packages until ready to use. Once they are opened, they will absorb moisture from the air, so reseal packages thoroughly if you must store a portion after opening. To make sure as little air as possible gets in the packages, I use rubber bands to secure them. Larger quantities of seaweed purchased in bulk may be stored in wide-mouthed jars with airtight seals. When stored away from moisture in a cool, dark place, dried seaweed can remain usable for many years.

Store each variety of seaweed separately, so their fragrances don't mingle. Label your jars until you are familiar with their appearance. With a little experience, you'll soon be able to tell hijiki from dulse as easily as you spot a zucchini among cucumbers.

These same guidelines apply for storing dried seaweed condiments and snacks. Store unused portions of pickled seaweed condiments in the refrigerator and use within a few days.

If a sea vegetable looks wilted or soggy, it has likely been exposed to moisture and will still be usable, if not as vibrant.

Cleaning

Sea vegetables do not need to be cleaned like land plants to remove dirt, since they have been well rinsed of saltwater, sand, and seashells before being dried. I do recommend the following quick, but thorough, cleaning to eliminate possible vestiges of these items before you eat or cook seaweed.

Spread the dried sea vegetable on a light surface and pick out any bits of shell or sand. This process is much like checking legumes for small stones and bits of dirt.

Rinsing the sea vegetables under cool running water removes any excess salt and begins the rehydration process, restoring the sea plants to their natural, moist condition. Depending on the sea plant's hardiness, hold it in your hands or set it in a colander, and place it under slow-running cool water for four or five seconds, moving it around with your hand to clean it evenly. For more fragile varieties, like dulse, gently swish the seaweed in a bowl of cool water for four or five seconds and then remove it from the water immediately. Each recipe has specific rinsing instructions required for the variety used to produce the desired consistency.

Do *not* overrinse sea vegetables. It is better to err on the side of less rinsing than to risk overrinsing. While light rinsing removes debris, overrinsing robs these undersea treasures of their full rich flavor.

Soaking

Some recipes require that the seaweed be soaked, not just rinsed. Soaking will leach out more of the salt from the sea vegetables, allowing their sweetness and other complex flavors to predominate. Soaking also can be used to fully rehydrate the sea plants, returning them to their natural, underwater texture. Each recipe includes specific instructions for soaking when appropriate.

Avoid oversoaking sea vegetables. Like overrinsing, oversoaking can leach out flavors and ruin the texture. If you soaked the sea vegetable for the allotted time but are not yet ready for the next step in a recipe, do not let the seaweed continue to soak. Strain it and set it aside. If you soaked more seaweed than you planned to use, put it in a sealed container in the refrigerator until you are ready to use it, but for no longer than one or two days. Its flavor becomes slightly stronger the longer it is hydrated. Soaked, strained seaweed will have more sea flavor after it has been in the refrigerator for a day or two.

Since it is so easy to use dried sea vegetables, there is little reason to freeze sea vegetables. If frozen, they are likely to get freezer burn.

No special equipment is needed for soaking seaweed. Earthenware, glass, plastic, even metal bowls are fine. Don't pour the water off the seaweed; to remove it from the bowl, lift the seaweed from the water with your hands, tongs, a hand strainer, or straining spoon. This way any remaining sand will settle to the bottom of the bowl and none of the seaweed will be lost down the drain.

After rinsing and soaking, and in most cases before (in their dried form), seaweed is ready to eat uncooked. While not all are especially palatable in this simple rehydrated state, none absolutely requires cooking. So, nibble and taste away while you prepare your favorite sea vegetable recipes!

Bringing Out the Best

When cooking sea vegetables, which tend to be salty, the addition of something sweet enhances their flavor. Use sweetness like a seasoning. The principle here is the same as when preparing sweet treats: a pinch of sea salt rounds out and mellows strong sweet flavors. Sweeteners from the Asian pantry like rice syrup, a honey-like sweetener, as well as maple syrup, blend well with and draw out the flavor of sea vegetables. Fresh apple juice also pairs well with sea vegetables. As you continue your foray into seaweed cuisine, experiment and discover your own combinations that draw out their best flavors.

Meet the Sea Vegetables

Agar (AH-gar)

Agar, also called agar-agar, is a natural, flavorless gelatin, wonderful when used to "set up" beautiful fresh fruit and to present cool, light, and refreshing summer vegetable aspics.

Unlike animal-based instant gelatins that dissolve in water, flaked agar has to swell up first with liquid before it can be dissolved easily. Otherwise, it will turn into clear, sticky little pearls.

Always soak first, then slowly bring the agar flakes in the soaking liquid just to the boiling point. Lower the heat and simmer until the flakes are no longer visible. Stirring with a wire whisk helps break up any clumps, especially those that may adhere to the bottom or side of the pot.

When using agar in bar form, estimate each bar to equal about 3 tablespoons of agar flakes. This form requires a rinsing with warm water, rather than just covering with water to soak. While rinsing, squeeze the bar until it collapses. Tear it into 2-inch pieces and soak it in enough water to cover the pieces for 10 to 15 minutes. It will look translucent and become pliable. Add to the liquid you want molded. Gently bring to a boil, whisking frequently. Lower the heat to a simmer. Cook for 15 minutes or until totally dissolved.

Agar thickens as it cools, not during cooking. To test, place a tablespoonful of the agar mixture in a small bowl in the freezer for 10 minutes. Remove it and see how firm it is. I allow all dishes made with agar to stop steaming and cool on the countertop before placing them in the refrigerator to completely firm up.

Appearance/how to buy: Can be bought in three forms: bar, flakes, and powder. Bars 10 by 1 inch are white, slightly translucent, and sold in packages of two. Flakes are gray-white, and are sold in 1-ounce packages (also called Kanten Flakes by Mitoku).

The powder is cream colored and is sold like spices in bulk by Frontier. I prefer not to cook with agar in powder form for two reasons: first, commercial processing of agar powder requires the use of sulphuric acid to dissolve the starches. Bleaches and dyes are used to neutralize color and flavor. Second, powdered agar yields a much tougher gelatin. Better to leave this form for industrial, commercial use.

Characteristics: Gelatinous, flavorless, agar swells up when soaked, then dissolves easily when heated. It gels only after it is no longer steaming and becomes a firmer gel as it gets colder.

Culinary uses: For gelatin desserts or vegetable aspics.

Preparation: Rinse agar bar under warm running water until soft, about 30 seconds, then tear it into 2-inch pieces. Soak for 15 minutes to dissolve.

Dissolve agar flakes by soaking for 15 minutes in water at room temperature.

After soaking, heat both forms gently, stirring frequently with a wire whisk while dissolving continues, about 10 minutes.

Nutritional values: Calcium, phosphorus; no calories.

Alaria (ah-LAR-ree-yah) or Wild Atlantic Wakame

Alaria, a salty variety of wakame, is harvested off the east coast of the United States. It requires thorough rinsing and soaking. In most dishes, it is best to soak it for 30 minutes, pour off the soaking liquid, rinse, and soak another 30 minutes. Cooking alaria with other ingredients mellows its flavor. It can be used interchangeably with wakame. When substituting for wakame, use one-third less alaria. To use it in recipes that do not require cooking, soak overnight, then rinse with cool water to refresh it.

Appearance/how to buy: Long strips, 1 to 2 inches wide, folded in a 2-ounce package by Maine Coast Sea Vegetable Company, Rising Tide, and others (See Mail-Order Sources, pages 124 and 125).

Characteristics: Robust and salty. Smooth; chewier than wakame.

Culinary uses: Great for soups, stews, casseroles, toasted condiments.

Preparation: Use scissors to cut the needed amount. Rinse under cool running water for 2 to 3 minutes. Soak in water for 30 minutes to overnight, depending on use. Rinse twice after soaking to minimize its strong flavor.

Nutritional values: Vitamins A, B, and C, iron, magnesium, iodine, fluoride, chromium, calcium, zinc.

Arame (AIR-a-may)

Arame is mild in flavor and cooks quickly. Its delicate strands must soak only about 5 minutes, otherwise its flavor will quickly be released into the soaking water. Even when the soaking water is used along with arame in preparing a dish, oversoaked arame will still taste bland.

I season arame with tamari or shoyu. Mirin and rice syrup, a honey-like sweetener made from brown rice, are also good seasoning complements. Season arame early in the cooking process, then add more seasoning during the last 5 to 10 minutes. The result is a richer, not saltier, flavor.

Add cooked arame to vegetables, grains, and burgers. As a topping, whether prepared specifically for that purpose or a quick use for leftovers, arame is a sure party pleaser.

Appearance/how to buy: Thin, black, threadlike strands. Comes in 1.75-ounce packages by Mitoku and in bulk from some health food stores.

Characteristics: Dry, brittle, but tender once soaked. Rich deep salty-sweet flavor. The longer it cooks, the more tender it becomes.

Culinary uses: Sautés, stir-fries, casseroles, stews, salads.

Preparation: Requires quick, light rinsing and 5 minutes of soaking in cool water at room temperature. Avoid oversoaking. Once arame is shiny and soft, drain the water. Can be used once soaked, or cooked further.

Nutritional values: Calcium, iodine, potassium, vitamin A, niacin, iron.

Shoyu, Tamari, Mirin

Shoyu, a fermented Japanese sauce that contains wheat, is lighter than tamari. Shoyu, tamari, and the many other varieties of "soy sauce" are interchangeable in most recipes. If you are using tamari in place of shoyu, use one-third less than the recipe calls for. Shoyu is sold in many markets, most health food stores, and in Japanese markets. When buying it, look for brands that contain no alcohol, preservatives, and artificial coloring. They taste awful! Tamari, traditional Japanese soy sauce made without wheat, has a rich, deep, strong flavor.

Mirin, a cooking wine made from rice, imparts a delicate sweetness and sheen.

Bullwhip Kelp

Bullwhip kelp, extraordinarily beautiful when growing in the sea, can become up to 50 yards long. The long blades are attached to a bulb that floats on the surface of the water, connected to a long, thick stipe—the stem of a sea plant. The edible portions are the blades and bulb. Loved for its crunchiness, bullwhip kelp easily absorbs moisture and loses its crunch. To restore the texture, place the kelp on a baking sheet and heat for 5 minutes in a 275°F oven.

Appearance/how to buy: Bright green, brittle, large flat pieces. Currently available by the ounce only by mail order. (See Rising Tide in Mail-Order Sources, page 125.)

Characteristics: Crunchy. Salty and sweet. Quickly becomes very tender when added to any warm food.

Culinary uses: Crumble and mix with currants and nuts for snacks, add to pasta dishes, mix into beans and stews during the final minutes of cooking.

Preparation: Use as is. No need to soak.

Nutritional values: Iodine, bromine, phosphorus, potassium, magnesium, iron, and trace elements.

Dulse

This rich, robust, salty seaweed can be used straight out of the package—but will be saltier—on salads, hot cereals, and grains. It can also be toasted or baked and will become less salty and bacon-like in flavor. Crumble it onto any food where crunch and salt is desired. After a quick wipe with a damp sponge to remove any tiny shells or sea life that may be attached in the folds, toast or bake for 5 to 7 minutes in a low (250°F) oven. Watch carefully; it will burn easily and become unusable. When lightly and quickly toasted, dulse will turn from its original deep purple-burgundy color to a medium brown. Resembling mild bacon in crunchiness and flavor, dulse is good for topping warm porridge, as a raw

salad condiment, a sandwich filler, and as a flavor enhancer for noodle dishes. A fun way to introduce this tasty, crunchy treat is to crush it well and sprinkle it over fresh popcorn.

Another way to prepare dulse is to run cold water over its folds for 5 seconds; it will be refreshed—tender and ready to be torn apart easily or lightly chopped. After refreshing, dulse may be added to the top of a salad for added flavor and nutrients.

Appearance/how to buy: Deep purple-burgundy. Small, crumbled, and irregularly folded bundles, varying in size from 3 to 6 inches long, in 2-ounce packages from Maine Coast Sea Vegetable Company and others (See Mail-Order Sources, pages 124 and 125). Dulse also comes ready to use as a condiment in shaker bottles, plain or with dried garlic, and is available in bulk from some health food stores. It is also sold smoked with applewood.

Characteristics: Slightly damp and crumpled. Very salty. Soft when lightly rinsed. Becomes super crunchy in minutes when toasted in oven or skillet (see above). Becomes soft and dissolves when added to soups or casseroles.

Culinary uses: Can be eaten raw as a topping sprinkled on soups, salads, and popcorn; toasted in sandwiches or as a substitute for bacon bits; or, after light rinsing, cooked in stews or casseroles.

Preparation: Requires careful sorting to remove tiny sand or shells in the folds. Depending on use, wipe dulse with a damp cloth or quickly rinse it under cool running water to refresh.

Nutritional values: Excellent source of vitamin C, calcium, iron, iodine, phosphorus, potassium, vitamins B_1, B_2.

Fucus Tips (FEW-cus) or Bladderwrack

Fucus tips were historically used as a tea. They are delicious when boiled in water with tamari and whole garlic cloves.

Appearance/how to buy: 3- to 4-inch, deep green, dry strands, with bumpy-looking surface, ½ inch wide. Currently available by the ounce only by mail order. (See Rising Tide in Mail-Order Sources, page 125.)

Characteristics: Tender, mild, sweet sea flavor. Chewy and maintains its chewy consistency in fast-cooking dishes.

Culinary uses: Excellent in quick-cooking dishes. If used for long-cooking dishes, it will become gelatinous and can help thicken soups and stews. Delicious in tempura, where it maintains its original dried, crispy texture.

Preparation: Rinse under cool running water for 1 minute, then soak for 20 minutes.

Nutritional values: Magnesium, protein, vitamins A, C, K, and E, iodine, bromine, zinc, iron, potassium.

Grapestone

Grapestone is a red algae that becomes creamier and creamier the longer it cooks. In Iceland, it was eaten as a sweetened pudding, cooked with flour and water and served with fresh cream.

Appearance/how to buy: Deep red/purple, slightly transparent color. Coarse surface, stretchy consistency. Wavy, irregular 2- to 3-inch pieces. Currently available by the ounce only by mail order. (See Rising Tide in Mail-Order Sources, page 125.)

Characteristics: Mild sea-salty flavor. Chewy and slippery when wet. Becomes creamy as it cooks. Its color is radically transformed by soaking and cooking—when heated 5 minutes, its purple fades to light brown.

Culinary uses: Any dish where creaminess is desired, for example, soups, side dishes, and sauces.

Preparation: Rinse under cool running water for 1 to 2 minutes. Then soak in cool water for 10 minutes. Drain immediately to maintain firm texture.

Nutritional values: Vitamin C and trace elements.

Hijiki (he-JEE-key)

Hijiki is one of the best nondairy sources of calcium available. It has a strong character that is tamed by soaking it a minimum of 20 minutes and discarding the soaking water or cooking it in apple juice, which mellows the deep flavor that often discourages newcomers to this powerful sea vegetable. It may sound like an odd combination, but the final product has no distinct apple flavor. I found that my family would eat twice the amount of hijiki when I cooked it in apple juice.

Hijiki is delicious with such strong seasonings as sautéed garlic, shallots, ginger, shoyu, and tamari. Since this sea vegetable is tougher and thicker and has a more robust flavor than most of the others, introduce it to new palates by chopping it finely and adding it to other dishes simply as an ingredient. With its pronounced dark color and shine, it adds color and texture to burgers, quiches, and stir-fries. It also makes a good side dish, once its taste is familiar; with its striking color and texture, it can take center stage on anyone's plate.

Appearance/how to buy: Thick, long, dry, black strands. Comes in 1.75-ounce packages from Mitoku and other companies.

Characteristics: Coarse and brittle before soaking. Thicker and flexible after soaking. Triples in volume after rinsing and soaking. One of the strongest flavors and cooking smells of all seaweed.

Culinary uses: Works well in long-cooked vegetable dishes, casseroles, and pâtés, and marinated in salads. Can be chopped finely and mixed into burgers, quiches, and stir-fries.

Preparation: Requires 20 to 30 minutes of soaking time for best flavor and at least 40 minutes of cooking time for tenderness.

Nutritional values: Excellent source of calcium, especially useful for strict vegetarians. Iron, iodine, phosphorus, potassium, vitamins A, B_2, niacin.

Irish Moss

Long associated with Ireland, often referred to as carageenan (from the coastal town Carragheen), this small bushlike red algae plant thrives on both sides of the Atlantic in colder waters and grows up to a foot high, covering rocks and other surfaces. It has been revered for centuries for its gelling quality and used mostly for commercial purposes. Irish moss has a salty, sulphur flavor and is difficult in small quantities for cooking.

Irish moss is the oldest seaweed used in industry. Boston breweries used it as a clarifying agent to bond with impurities in large vats. The impurities would rise to the top where they could be siphoned off.

Appearance/how to buy: Purplish, slightly transparent flakes. Sold in bulk and with spices from Frontier.

Characteristics: Spongy. Distinct salty, sulphur flavor. Requires lengthy cooking, approximately 1 hour, to become soft and pliable. Gelatinous when cooked.

Culinary uses: Thickens hearty soups and stews.

Preparation: Check for tiny shells and other dried sea life and remove them before rinsing. You can drop pieces directly into your cooking pot.

Nutritional values: High in vitamin A, iodine, iron, sodium, phosphorus, magnesium, calcium, copper.

Kombu (COME-boo)

Note: An Atlantic Ocean variety is called kelp. It is more tender in texture but slightly stronger in taste.

Kombu is the king of seaweed. Its leathery, shiny appearance misleads—it is not tough. It will, however, withstand long cooking before it dissolves. Its mild, moderately salty flavor makes it ideal to enhance soup, stocks, and stews, and it is a wonderful aid to digesting bean dishes. Kiri Kombu is kombu that has been cut into long, thin strands. Boil or simmer it for 15 to 60 minutes and then remove it from the pot. Slice pieces of cooked kombu super thin and put them back into the soup or stew, or save them for up to 2 days and re-use in a vegetable dish.

Rinse kombu before cooking under cool running water and then place in a bowl with water to cover. Avoid oversoaking. Do not let kombu soak after it has expanded to 2 to 3 times its dried-state size, usually 15 minutes. If oversoaking occurs, kombu will become gelatinous and too slippery to grip and cut easily. If the whole piece is to be added to a stew, this slippery texture is nothing to be concerned about. I often add the soaking water to the dish I am preparing if the recipe calls for liquid.

Unless kombu is cooked for an hour, it is quite chewy. Let whole pieces of it dissolve in stews, or cut it finely so it cooks thoroughly in a shorter amount of time. Kombu seldom takes center stage, except when pickled.

I enjoy using it as a decorative garnish for dishes in which it has been cooked. Its unique texture and durability make it beautiful on a serving platter. Use a super sharp knife to cut elegant, long strips for presentation.

Appearance/how to buy: Thick 3-inch-wide, deep-green strips. There are many brands with various size packages, including 2-ounce packages and 2.75-ounce packages of flakes from Maine Coast Sea Vegetable Company. It can also be bought in bulk from some health food stores and by mail order.

Characteristics: Dry and brittle before soaking; smooth and leathery after soaking. Fragrantly salty. Flexible and expands from 2 to 3 times its original (dried-state) size after rinsing and soaking. Dissolves after 90 minutes of cooking.

Culinary uses: Excellent flavor enhancer, natural "MSG" source. Use as a seasoning for soup stocks, stews, and long-cooking vegetable dishes. Helps soften beans during cooking and reduces the flatulence and bloating they can produce.

Preparation: Rinse under cool running water and soak for 5 to 10 minutes.

Nutritional values: Calcium, iron, iodine, phosphorus, potassium, vitamins A, B_2, niacin, vitamin C.

Laver (Wild Nori)

Wild nori is harvested from both the Atlantic (top) in Ireland, Wales, and Maine, and from the Pacific (bottom) in northern California. It resembles Japanese cultivated nori in its sweetness. It has a unique crunch both raw and cooked. The Pacific variety is a bit translucent and less salty than the Atlantic harvest, which is saltier and more dense. It was used by many aboriginal peoples in North America, especially in Alaska, where it was cooked with fish.

Appearance/how to buy: Pacific variety is black-purple with a translucent quality, and milder in flavor than the Atlantic variety, which is gray-black and slightly stronger. It can be bought in 1-ounce packages from Maine Coast Sea Vegetable Company. It is also available in bulk from some health food stores.

Characteristics: Chewy with a slight crunch. Sweet flavor. After soaking 15 minutes, laver is crunchy and a little slippery. Even after boiling, it maintains its crunch.

Culinary uses: Tremendously versatile. Good in salads, snacks, and soups.

Preparation: Can be eaten right out of the package, soaked, or cooked and still maintains its texture.

Nutritional values: High in vitamins A and C.

Nori (NOR-ee)

Most nori is cultivated and processed into the flat sheets most widely recognized as the covering for sushi. Nori can also be used in place of crackers. Simply tear the sheets in half or cut into squares with scissors and use like a wrap to pick up bite-size quantities of food. Its crunchy, sweet, lightly salty flavor is a great munchie. Nori is also excellent for giving leftovers a quick lift. Invent new combinations of noodles, grains, and vegetables and spread them on a sheet of nori. Roll it all up with a sushi mat and instantly you have fun, delicious snacks, lunches,

and picnic treats. A quick dinner at my house sometimes consists of setting the table with sheets of nori, condiments, grains, vegetables, and several bamboo mats. Everyone assembles their own rolls. It's quick to set up, especially when there are leftovers. A few fresh raw ingredients such as scallions, watercress, avocado, and carrots give the leftovers vitality and freshness.

Appearance/how to buy: Crispy black-green sheets, toasted or untoasted. Sheets come in a wide variety, ranging from 7 and 10 sheets to 50 sheets, in 3.5-ounce, 6-ounce, or 9-ounce packages. The sheets come with creases 1¼ inch apart. Generally the toasted nori comes in packages of fewer sheets. There are numerous nori producers, and nori is often available in better grocery stores. Nori is also available in precut 1-inch strips from Health Flavors! Nori can also be bought in shaker condiment form, sometimes mixed with seeds and spices.

Characteristics: Slightly sweet, delicate flavor. Sheets are more flexible and a deep-green-black before toasting and crunchier and green-brown after toasting. Softens and dissolves quickly when cooked.

Culinary uses: Most commonly used as the covering for the rice in Japanese sushi rolls. It is an excellent snack right out of the package. It can be added to soups, where it will soften and dissolve quickly and easily. It is wonderful alongside noodles, grains, and vegetables and can be cooked into a paste for a condiment dish.

Preparation: Can be bought and eaten right away. Can be toasted or left untoasted. No washing or soaking is required.

Nutritional values: Calcium, iron, phosphorus, vitamins A, B_2, niacin, vitamin C.

Sea Lettuce

A bright green, pungent-flavored sea vegetable used mostly as a condiment, sea lettuce is harvested off both coasts of North America, as well as in other oceans. It is often found in the same locations as nori. It is not the most widely used seaweed for culinary purposes, having a very pungent flavor best suited for condiments where a small amount goes a long way.

Appearance/how to buy: Crinkled, olive green, packed tightly in bags. Currently available by the ounce only by mail order. (See Rising Tide and Mendocino Sea Vegetable Company in Mail-Order Sources, pages 124 and 125.)

Characteristics: Chewy when dried. Soft when heated with liquid or steamed. Pungent flavor. When quickly rinsed and soaked for 5 minutes, its color brightens and it becomes transparent and less pungent.

Culinary uses: As a condiment for grains and vegetables when dried. Can be added to marinated salads after soaking. A garnish for stir-fries.

Preparation: Use straight from the package. Has no surface salt that requires rinsing.

Nutritional values: Protein, iodine, manganese, potassium, magnesium, niacin, and vitamins A, B_1, B_2nd C. High in iron.

Sea Palm

Sea palm grows only along the northern Pacific coast of North America. It resembles miniature palm trees, secured to rocks and cliffs along the water's edge. It grows up to 2 feet tall, with each plant having 40 to 80 long olive-green blades of seaweed. The plants are incredibly strong and able to withstand constant pounding from the waves during incoming tides.

Because its flavor is so subtle, it is adaptable to almost any kind of seasoning. Its texture is the most unusual of all seaweed. Its appearance is like pasta. It can withstand long cooking without disintegrating.

Appearance/how to buy: Looks like spinach pasta. Currently available by the ounce only by mail order. (See Rising Tide in Mail-Order Sources, page 125.)

Characteristics: Sturdy, easy-to-handle strands. Holds up well in long-cooking dishes. Mild flavor. Soaking yields beautiful ribbon-like strands that hold up to long cooking times.

Culinary uses: As a snack right out of the package. Toasted and crushed onto warm foods for a garnish or an added flavorful crunch.

Preparation: Soak for 20 minutes.

Nutritional values: High in bromine and trace elements.

Wakame (Wa-KAMAY)

Wakame, familiar to many because it is often used in miso soup, is among the more sweet-tasting sea vegetables. It can be eaten raw, after rinsing and soaking, and requires little preparation for most dishes. It has a silky, visually appealing texture that makes it easy to introduce to unfamiliar palates. Wakame's delicate taste makes this vegetable easy to include in a variety of dishes. Ito wakame is a lighter green and more delicate.

Either wipe wakame with a clean, damp sponge or quickly rinse it under cold water to remove excess sea salt and dust. Place it in a small bowl and cover with fresh cool water. Use only enough water to submerge the pieces. Excess water will leach all the flavor and minerals. Within 5 to 7 minutes the wakame will swell and be tender. After soaking, wakame increases to twice its original size. Remove from the soaking water. Do not oversoak. (Sometimes I save the soaking water and add it to a soup. The liquid can be saved for a day or two covered in the refrigerator). If a piece of wakame is more than an inch wide, you may need to use shorter pieces than the recipe calls for.

After cooking a minimum of 20 minutes, it will break up and dissolve into very tiny pieces. Only attractive tiny flecks of green remain, and this is wonderful for light-colored dishes where you may want the health-giving qualities of a sea vegetable without the large, dark pieces of seaweed that would make the dish unappetizing.

Sometimes the midrib or stem of the wakame remains in one piece after cooking. This piece is tough, chewy, and requires a longer cooking time. If you don't want it to be part of your dish, you may cut it out with a knife after soaking the wakame and let it cook prior to adding the soft pieces to the dish, or you may remove it from the cooked dish, finely chop it, and return it to the dish, or you may remove it and save it to add to another dish. It will keep for a day or two in the refrigerator.

Appearance/how to buy: Crispy, dark green. Comes in 1- to 2-inch wide strips of varying lengths, typically 4 to 6 inches. Packaging varies, but 2-ounce bags are most common. It is sometimes sold in bulk at health food stores, and bulk bags can contain strips 12 inches or longer.

Characteristics: Silky flexible strips after soaking. Delicate, mild flavor. Softens quickly and dissolves into small pieces in 20 minutes of cooking.

Culinary uses: Great in soups or when lightly toasted, baked, marinated, or eaten raw after soaking.

Preparation: Rinse under cool water. Soak for 5 minutes.

Nutritional values: Calcium, iron, iodine, phosphorus, potassium, vitamins A, B_1, B_2.

Appetizers
and Meal Starters

The arame brings a light sea flavor to the eggplant and other vegetables.

This rich appetizer can be followed by a lighter meal of poached fish with couscous and vegetables.

Arame-Stuffed Eggplants

Makes 4 servings

½ cup pine nuts

6 baby eggplants, halved lengthwise, stalks left on

2 tablespoons extra virgin olive oil

1 medium red onion, cut in ½-inch dice

1½ cups cremini mushrooms, coarsely chopped

4 garlic cloves, coarsely chopped

½ cup lightly packed arame, rinsed

2 tomatoes, coarsely chopped

¼ cup finely chopped flat-leaf parsley

2 teaspoons sea salt

1. Preheat oven to 350°F.

2. Toast the pine nuts by heating them in a small, heavy skillet, over low heat, stirring constantly. No oil is needed because of their high oil content. They will become light brown within 5 minutes. Remove from the pan immediately, as they burn easily. Set aside to cool.

3. Place the eggplant halves in a large skillet, cover with boiling water, and cook over medium heat until just tender, 3 to 4 minutes. Drain and set aside. Once the eggplant has cooled, scoop out the flesh with a teaspoon, leaving the shells intact. Chop the flesh coarsely and reserve. Lightly oil a baking dish and place the shells on it.

4. Heat the oil in the skillet for 15 seconds and add the onion. Cook over medium heat for several minutes until golden brown. Add the mushrooms, stirring frequently until moisture is released and they begin to brown. Add the garlic and arame, mixing well, and continue cooking for 5 minutes or until the garlic is fragrant and the arame well mixed in.

5. Stir in the tomatoes, reserved eggplant, all but a tablespoon of the pine nuts, and the parsley. Cook for 2 minutes, then add the salt. Adjust the seasoning if needed. Remove from the heat. Spoon the filling into the eggplant shells. Garnish with the remaining pine nuts and bake for 10 minutes.

Serve on individual plates, two halves per person. For a platter presentation, line the eggplants vertically, side by side, with stems at the top.

This is a wonderful crunch and munch kelp snack. The kelp maintains its shape when fried in the hot oil and will be crispy deep brown with a rich salty flavor.

Kelp Chips with Horseradish Dip

Makes 4 servings

Four 6-inch pieces kelp

⅓ cup sesame oil

3 carrots, cut into 4-inch strips

½ head broccoli,
cut into 3-inch florets

For the dip

1 cup whole milk yogurt

1½ tablespoons prepared horseradish

1 tablespoon rice syrup

2 teaspoons lemon juice

3 cups unsalted corn chips

1. Remove excess salt from the kelp by moistening a paper towel and quickly wiping the pieces. Be careful not to get the kelp soggy. Using scissors, cut the kelp pieces in half lengthwise and again crosswise.

2. Heat the oil in a skillet over medium heat. Add the kelp strips to the hot oil and fry for 3 minutes on each side, or until they change to a deep golden-brown color. Remove and drain on paper towels.

3. Boil a quart of water in a saucepan and blanch the carrots for 2 minutes. With a slotted spoon, remove them from the water and set aside. Blanch the broccoli for 3 minutes or until bright green, and set aside.

4. In a small serving bowl whisk the dip ingredients together.

To serve, set the dip bowl in the center of a platter and alternate the kelp and corn chips around it. Surround the chips with the carrots and broccoli.

Soda bread uses baking powder and baking soda rather than yeast for leavening. Instead of the traditional caraway seeds, I use dulse flakes, a traditional seaweed of Ireland, to spice it up. I prefer muffins to round loaves because they bake faster and are easy for lunches, travel, and little hands.

These can be served with strawberry or other flavored butters. They make a great accompaniment to hot bean soups.

Dulse-Filled Irish Soda Muffins

Makes 12 muffins

2¼ cups unbleached all-purpose flour
2 teaspoons baking powder
¼ teaspoon baking soda
½ teaspoon sea salt
½ cup maple sugar crystals
¾ cup currants
1 tablespoon dulse flakes
1 egg
1 cup whole milk yogurt
¼ cup sunflower oil

1. Preheat the oven to 400°F. Lightly oil 12 paper muffin cups and place into the muffin pan.

2. Whisk together the flour, baking powder, baking soda, salt, maple sugar crystals, currants, and dulse flakes in a bowl.

3. In another bowl, whisk together the egg, yogurt, and oil.

4. Quickly and gently combine the wet and dry ingredients with a few stirs of a rubber spatula. Do not overmix or the muffins will be tough.

5. Spoon the batter into the muffin cups, filling them ⅔ full. Bake for 15 minutes or until lighly golden. Remove from the oven and place on a wire rack to cool.

Variation

Add ½ cup chopped walnuts, almonds, or sunflower seeds.

My children say this ribbon-like seaweed dish looks like spinach pasta. Serve it on small plates with steamed broccoli, or with a small square of warm polenta and a sprinkling of chopped red bell pepper, or by itself.

The tender texture combined with the graceful and hardy appearance of sea palm reminds me of the ebb and flow of the sea.

California Sea Palm with Polenta

Makes 4 servings

2½ cups loosely packed
dried sea palm

2 tablespoons extra virgin olive oil

2 shallots, thinly sliced

2½ tablespoons tamari

½ teaspoon sea salt

1 tablespoon butter

10 large cloves garlic, thinly sliced

3 tablespoons honey

For the polenta

¾ teaspoon sea salt

1 cup corn grits

chopped red bell pepper

1. Rinse the sea palm by stirring it in a bowl of cool water for 3 seconds. Drain. Repeat. Place the sea palm in the bowl with cool water to cover. Soak for 20 minutes. Lift the sea palm from the soaking water with your hands, place it in another bowl, and set aside.

2. Heat the oil in a skillet. Add the shallots and saute for 3 minutes until they are browned and softened. Add the sea palm and sauté for 5 minutes. The sea palm should be well coated with oil.

3. Add 1½ cups water, tamari, salt, and butter. Bring just to a boil, then lower the flame, cover, and simmer for 15 minutes.

4. Add the garlic and simmer uncovered for 10 minutes. The liquid should start reducing. Avoid too high a flame so that the sea palm does not over-cook and become mushy. Add the honey and simmer for 10 more minutes. Very little moisture should be left. The sea palm will look tender and slightly creamy.

5. Lightly grease a small baking sheet. In a saucepan, bring 3 cups water and the salt to a boil. Slowly whisk in the corn grits and continue to whisk constantly until thickened, about 10 minutes. Lower the flame and continue whisking for 15 minutes. The mixture will be very thick.

6. Pour the hot polenta mixture onto the sheet. Spread the mixture with a wet spatula into a ½-inch layer. As it cools, it will stiffen. Once it's completely firm, about 45 minutes, cut the polenta into squares. Serve immediately. If it cools, it can be warmed in a 300°F oven for 10 minutes.

To serve the sea palm with the polenta, cut a 4-inch square of firm polenta for each plate and place ½ cup of cooked sea palm in the center of the square. Garnish with a dash of the chopped red bell pepper.

Cooking robust hijiki with apple juice tempers its strong flavor. Mirin, a rice cooking wine available in Asian markets and whole food stores, imparts a delicate sweetness and sheen to the hijiki.

The hijiki will become a deeper black color when cooked. Chopped finely and placed on individual crostinis, topped with a dollop of sour cream, the hijiki resembles caviar in appearance but with a sea vegetable saltiness in flavor.

Hijiki Crostini

Makes 15 to 20 crostini

1 cup dried hijiki

2 tablespoons toasted sesame oil

7 shallots, minced

3 cups apple juice, enough to cover the seaweed by 1 inch

2 tablespoons mirin

3 tablespoons tamari

Juice of ½ lemon

Baguette, thinly sliced

1 cup sour cream

1 bunch chives, very finely chopped

1. Rinse the hijiki by stirring it in a bowl of cool water for 3 seconds. Drain. Repeat. Cover the hijiki in the bowl with 4 cups of cool water. Soak for 20 minutes. Lift the hijiki from the soaking water with your hands, squeeze, and finely chop.

2. Heat the sesame oil in a skillet. Sauté the shallots for 3 to 5 minutes, until softened and lightly browned. Add the chopped hijiki, apple juice, mirin, and tamari.

3. Bring to a boil, then reduce to a simmer and cook for 40 minutes, or until the liquid is absorbed. Toward the end of the cooking time, stir to help evaporate any remaining liquid. The hijiki will be shiny. Add the lemon juice.

4. Cool the mixture to room temperature or refrigerate, if preparing ahead. Place a tablespoon of the mixture on a baguette slice. Place a dollop of sour cream in the center and a dash of chives on top. Repeat with the remaining ingredients. (The hijiki can be prepared a day ahead of time. Take it out of the refrigerator an hour prior to serving to remove the chill. It is best served at room temperature.)

Soups
and Stews

When Taiwanese fishermen are out at sea, they prepare a pot of soup with freshly caught fish and sea vegetables. Quick, simple, and delicate, this more simplified version of their clear soup uses arame for its fast cooking and mild flavor. Serve with hearty bread for dipping.

Taiwanese Fishermen's Soup

Makes 4 servings

½ cup lightly packed arame

2 large onions, cut into 1-inch pieces

2 parsnips, peeled and cut into ½-inch rounds

1 potato, peeled and cut into 1-inch pieces

1½ pounds fish fillets such as sole, flounder, or scrod; cut into four 3-inch pieces

2 teaspoons sea salt, or to taste

¼ cup chopped basil

6 sprigs sweet basil

1. Rinse the arame in cool water for 10 seconds. Place the arame in a bowl, cover with water, and soak for 5 minutes. Lift the seaweed out with your hands and finely chop. Set aside.

2. In a Dutch oven or soup pot combine 8 cups water, the onions, parsnips, and potato and bring to a boil. Reduce the heat and simmer for 20 minutes. The soup should be creamy and the vegetables soft.

3. Add the fish and arame to the pot. Simmer for 10 minutes, until the fish is tender and falling apart.

4. Turn off the heat. Add the salt and basil and stir well. Adjust the seasoning if needed. Serve garnished with the basil sprigs.

Sea palm adds texture and flavor to long-cooking stews. Its unique ribbon-like quality and appearance when cooked is similar to spinach fettucine. Sauerkraut (from a jar or plastic package, not a can) and apple juice impart the sour and sweet flavors to the vegetables. Serve with brown basmati rice.

In dried form, sea palm strands are 4 to 6 inches in length. Measure in a glass measuring cup. Rather than packing it down, let the sea palm rest in the measuring cup and estimate the measure.

Sweet-and-Sour Sea Palm Stew

Makes 4 servings

2 cups sea palm

2 tablespoons canola oil

3 red onions, quartered

2 carrots, cut into 2-inch chunks

1 parsnip, cut into 2-inch chunks

1 small rutabaga,
cut into 2-inch chunks (remove
any wax with a peeler or knife)

2 cups sauerkraut (from a jar),
juice reserved

1½ cups apple juice

1 tablespoon tamari

1. Place the sea palm in a bowl and fill the bowl with cool water. Using your fingers, stir for 10 seconds. Drain off the water. Refill the bowl with fresh water to completely cover the sea palm. Let the sea palm soak for 15 minutes and lift it out with your hands. Set aside.

2. Heat the oil in a Dutch oven or stew pot for 20 seconds. Add the onions, stir, and coat well with the oil. Sauté for 5 minutes until the edges are slightly brown.

3. Layer the carrots, parsnip, and rutabaga over the onions, without mixing. Put the sea palm over the layered vegetables. Spread the sauerkraut over the sea palm. Pour 1 cup of the sauerkraut juice and the apple juice into the pot. Bring the liquid to a boil and cook uncovered for 5 minutes. Add the tamari. Lower the heat and simmer covered for 35 to 45 minutes. Do not stir while cooking. The vegetables will become very soft, the sea palm tender and slightly chewy. A small amount of liquid should remain in the pot.

4. Remove from the heat. Toss the ingredients in the pot. Divide among 4 soup bowls, making sure each serving includes some of the tasty liquid.

Miso soup, eaten daily in Japan, always contains a tender, mild sea vegetable, usually wakame. Miso soup is simple, with only wakame and scallions, or with added onion, carrot, winter squash, and tofu. It should be sweet rather than salty. Miso is revered as a digestive aid.

Finely chopped fresh greens added while simmering the miso gives it variety in presentation and flavor.

White miso can be purchased in the refrigerated section of most Asian markets as well as in health food stores. If you wish, substitute Bonito and Kombu Stock (page 49) for the water.

Classic Miso Soup

Makes 4 servings

5 dried shiitakes

4-inch strip wakame, rinsed, soaked, drained, and finely chopped

1 onion, thinly sliced

1 carrot, cut into matchsticks

2 tablespoons white miso

½ pound silken tofu, cut into ½-inch cubes

3-inch piece fresh ginger or 1 tablespoon ginger juice

¼ cup chopped scallions

1. Lightly rinse the mushrooms under warm running water for 10 seconds. Soak them in 1 cup warm water until soft, about 15 minutes. Drain, cut off the tough stems, and slice the mushrooms thinly. Place the mushrooms, wakame, onion, and carrot in a Dutch oven or soup pot with 7 cups water. Bring to a boil. Reduce the heat, cover, and simmer for 15 minutes.

2. Place the miso in a small bowl and add ¼ cup of the broth from the vegetables. Using a fork, stir the miso and broth until the mixture is a smooth paste. Add the miso and tofu to the pot.

3. Grate the ginger on a fine grater. Squeeze the ginger pulp in the palm of your hand to extract the juice (discard the pulp). Add the juice to the pot. Stir and simmer for 5 minutes. Serve garnished with the scallions.

Smoked dulse adds a rich smoked pork flavor that contrasts with the mild flavor of the can-nellini beans. Also referred to as white kidney beans, cannellini are often used in Italian cook-ing for their soft, creamy texture. Any white bean will work. If you are short on time, use canned white beans. Drain and rinse them first, add the bay leaf, thyme, celery, and parsnip and pro-ceed to step 4.

Creamy White Bean Soup

Makes 4 servings

1½ cups cannellini beans, picked over, rinsed, and soaked overnight in 3 cups water

1 bay leaf

2 sprigs thyme

2 ribs celery, chopped into 1-inch pieces

1 parsnip, cut into 1-inch rounds

1 tablespoon extra virgin olive oil

½ tablespoon butter

1 large onion, cut into 1-inch pieces

2 red potatoes, peeled and cut into 1-inch pieces

3 medium tomatoes, peeled and finely chopped

2 tablespoons smoked dulse flakes

2 teaspoons sea salt, or to taste

Dash of black pepper

Olive oil to taste

1. Drain the beans and rinse with cool fresh water. Place the beans in a Dutch oven or soup pot with 6 cups of water. Bring to a boil and boil uncovered for 30 minutes.

2. Reduce the heat to a simmer, and add the bay leaf and thyme. Simmer uncovered for 1½ hours. With tongs, remove the bay leaf and thyme. Add the celery and parsnip.

3. Heat the oil and butter in a skillet over medium heat, and add the onion and potatoes, stirring frequently, until the onion starts to brown, about 5 minutes. The potatoes should be golden at the edges. Stir in the tomatoes and cook for 3 minutes. Add the potato-onion-tomato mixture to the beans. Mix well, adding the dulse flakes, salt, and pepper. Simmer for 15 minutes, or until all the ingredients are very soft. Ladle the soup into bowls and float a drizzle of olive oil on top of each serving.

Wakame becomes tender when simmered for several minutes; no prior soaking or cutting is required here. Once processed in a blender, the wakame adds subtle salty seasoning and bits of green to this creamy, bright orange, spicy-sweet soup.

If sweet potatoes are not available, yams are also excellent.

Curried Sweet Potato Soup

Makes 6 servings

2 tablespoons coconut oil

2 large onions, cut in ½-inch dice

2½ tablespoons curry powder

½ teaspoon cinnamon

½ teaspoon ground cardamom

6 medium sweet potatoes, peeled and cut into 2-inch pieces

3 Granny Smith apples, peeled and cut into 2-inch pieces

8-inch strip wakame, rinsed under cool running water for 3 seconds

Salt and black pepper to taste

12 fresh cilantro leaves

1. Heat the oil in a soup pot over low heat for 10 seconds. Sauté the onions until lightly browned, about 5 minutes. Stir in the curry powder, cinnamon, and cardamom. Mix well until the onions are coated with spices and release their fragrance, 2 to 3 minutes. Add the sweet potato and apples to the onion-spice mixture. Stir to coat well with the seasonings.

2. Place the wakame strip in the soup pot with 6 cups water. Bring to a boil. Lower the heat, cover the pot, and simmer for 40 minutes, or until the potatoes are tender when pierced with a fork. Using a slotted spoon, lift the potatoes and apples from the pot and place them in a blender, filling the container until half full. Pour in enough broth to blend easily. Avoid overfilling the blender, as hot soup may splash out.

3. Transfer the blended soup to a clean pot and season with salt and pepper to taste. Ladle into individual bowls and garnish each with 2 cilantro leaves.

Variations

Substitute vegetable stock for water. For an extra rich version, use 3 cups coconut milk and 3 cups water or vegetable stock. Alaria, the Atlantic variety of wakame, can also be used in this recipe. It is saltier and a bit tougher than arame and takes longer to soften. If substituting, use a 4-inch piece of alaria.

Alaria, a bit stronger in flavor and hardier in texture than wakame, gives this brothy soup a good, salty base for the winter vegetables, chicken, and colorful noodles to mingle with.

You can pound the chicken breasts following the instructions in this recipe or purchase them already pounded by a butcher.

Chicken Noodle Stew

Makes 4 servings

8-inch piece alaria

2 cups flat noodles

2 tablespoons corn oil

1 large onion, chopped

2 carrots, cut into 1-inch rounds

½ medium celery root, skin removed and cut into 2-inch squares

5 cloves garlic, thinly sliced

2 sprigs thyme

3 boneless, skinless chicken breasts

3 tablespoons tamari, or to taste

½ cup chopped flat-leaf parsley

1. Rinse the alaria in cool water for 5 seconds. Place in a bowl and cover with cool water to soak for 10 minutes. Lift out the alaria with your hands and chop into coarse pieces.

2. Boil 2 quarts of water in a Dutch oven or large soup pot and stir in the noodles. Cook until al dente, about 8 minutes. Quickly rinse. Drain and set aside.

3. Heat the oil in the pot over medium heat for 15 seconds. Add the onion and sauté until fragrant and transparent, about 2 minutes. Stir in the carrots, celery root, and garlic to coat the vegetables with oil. Pour 2 quarts water and the alaria and thyme into the pot.

4. Place the chicken breasts between two pieces of plastic wrap and pound with a meat pounder until the breasts are ½ inch thick. Cut the meat into 2-inch chunks. Add the chicken pieces to the pot and bring to a boil. Lower the heat to a simmer and cook until the chicken is no longer pink in the center, about 10 minutes.

5. Remove the thyme sprigs with tongs and add the cooked noodles and tamari. Simmer for 5 minutes. To serve, ladle the soup into bowls and garnish with lots of chopped parsley.

Refreshing lemongrass and ginger combine with two seafoods—shrimp and arame—for a spicy and warming soup. Arame has a mild saltiness and soft texture. Avoid oversoaking the arame, as all the flavor will leach out.

Lemongrass-Shrimp-Rice Soup

Makes 4 servings

2 stalks lemongrass

¾ cup lightly packed arame

¾ pound small shrimp, peeled, deveined, rinsed

6-inch piece fresh ginger or ⅓ cup ginger juice

3 tablespoons lemon juice

2 teaspoons coconut oil

3 shallots, minced

1 rib celery, minced

½ cup cooked basmati rice

1½ teaspoons sea salt

3 Napa cabbage leaves, cut in half lengthwise and shredded crosswise

¼ cup coarsely chopped cilantro

5 scallions, thinly sliced

1. Trim any tough or wilted outer leaves off the lemongrass. Cut the stalks into 4-inch lengths and smash lightly with the flat side of a knife. (This brings out the oils and releases the aromatic flavor.) Set aside.

2. Rinse the arame in a bowl of cool water for 5 seconds and drain well. Cover with cool water and soak for 10 minutes. Lift out the arame with your hands and set aside.

3. Place the shrimp in a bowl. Grate the ginger with a fine grater into another bowl. Squeeze the juice out of the pulp with your hands over the shrimp (discard the pulp). Add the lemon juice and toss well. Cover and refrigerate until needed.

4. Heat the oil in a Dutch oven or soup pot over medium heat for 15 seconds. Add the lemongrass, shallots, celery, and arame. Stir for 2 to 3 minutes, coating the vegetables with oil, until the shallots are lightly browned.

5. Pour in 5 cups water, the rice and salt and bring to a boil. Lower the heat and simmer for 15 minutes, or until the water is slightly starchy from the rice. Using tongs, remove the lemongrass and discard. Add the marinated shrimp with their juice and the cabbage and simmer for 3 to 5 minutes, or until the shrimp are pink and the cabbage leaves have wilted. Remove the pot from the heat and stir in the cilantro. Ladle the soup into serving bowls and garnish with the scallions.

Basmati rice

Rather than cook a small amount of grain for this and other recipes, I prepare enough rice for several days. This gives me a jump start for other dishes.

1 cup rice
2 cups water
Pinch of sea salt

Bring all the ingredients to a boil, lower the heat, and cook covered for 40 minutes. Remove from the heat and let sit for 5 minutes before removing the lid.

Wild nori can withstand long cooking times without disintegrating and maintains its crunch even after soaking and cooking. It adds a sweet flavor to this bean soup.

If fresh fava beans are unavailable, substitute frozen fava or lima beans and skip step 1.

Italian Fava Bean Soup

Makes 6 servings

2½ pounds fava beans in pods or 3 cups shelled beans

1 cup firmly packed wild nori

1 tablespoon extra virgin olive oil

1 tablespoon butter

3 shallots, minced

4 cloves garlic , minced

2 ribs celery, minced

1 small leek, thoroughly rinsed, thinly sliced

1 carrot, minced

1 tablespoon dried basil

1 teaspoon ground thyme

2 teaspoons dried oregano

1½ teaspoons sea salt

¼ cup chopped flat-leaf parsley plus 6 sprigs

1. In a Dutch oven or soup pot, bring 1 quart of water to a boil. Remove the fava beans from the pods. Add to the pot and boil 2 minutes, or until the skins are wrinkly and the beans are all floating on the surface of the water. Drain in a colander. When the beans have cooled, gently peel off the thick skin. The beans should be tender and bright green. Discard the skins. Set the beans aside.

2. Place the nori in a bowl and fill the bowl with cold water. Drain immediately. Add 1 cup water and the nori to the bowl. Let soften for 30 minutes.

3. Over low heat, warm the olive oil and butter in the pot for 30 seconds, or until the butter is melted. Add the shallots, stirring well. When the shallots are softened, about 5 minutes, add the garlic. Mix well for 1 minute. Avoid browning the garlic. Add the celery, leek, carrot, basil, thyme, oregano, and salt to the pot. Stir well.

4. Remove the nori from the water with your hands and gently squeeze out the excess water. Chop it into coarse pieces and add it to the soup pot. Pour 6 cups water into the pot. Bring to a boil, lower the heat, and simmer covered for 20 minutes. Stir in the fava beans and simmer for 10 minutes. Turn off the heat. Add the chopped parsley. Ladle into soup bowls and garnish with the parsley sprigs.

Bonito flakes, the shavings of dried and fermented bonito fish, have a deep smoky fish flavor.

In Japanese cooking, this stock intensifies flavors in soups, stews, and noodle broths. Enjoy the stock on its own or with your choice of sea salt, soy sauce, miso, or ginger. Fresh dashi lasts about one week in the refrigerator.

Add fresh seasonal vegetables as desired. Quick-cooking greens such as watercress, spinach, and Napa cabbage brighten the soup. Pour some dashi over cooked noodles for a quick meal. Or simmer chicken or tofu in the broth after the bonito is removed.

Bonito and Kombu Stock (Dashi)

Makes 1 quart

8-inch strip kombu
½ cup bonito flakes

1. Rinse the kombu under cool running water or wipe with a damp cloth.

2. In a soup pot, bring 1 quart of water and the kombu to a boil. Lower the heat and simmer for 15 minutes.

3. Remove the kombu and let it cool. Finely slice it and return it to the pot of stock.

4. Place the bonito flakes in a small strainer. Lower it into the pot for 3 to 5 minutes, until the flakes are softened. Remove the bonito and discard. If the bonito gets into the water, pour the water through a fine-mesh strainer to strain out the bonito.

Korean Wakame and Beef Soup

Makes 4 servings

2 tablespoons extra virgin olive oil

1¼ pounds stew beef,
cut into 2-inch chunks

½ cup lightly packed ito wakame

2 tablespoons peeled, minced ginger

¼ cup shoyu

½ pound button mushrooms,
thinly sliced

5 cloves garlic, thinly sliced

½ teaspoon cayenne pepper

1 teaspoon sea salt

6 scallions, thinly sliced

1. Heat 1 tablespoon of the oil in a skillet, add the beef, and sear all sides. Using tongs, turn the pieces after 5 minutes, or when well browned. Remove from the skillet and set aside. Add ¼ cup water to the hot skillet and deglaze, using with a wooden spoon to loosen all the delicious bits stuck to the pan. Reserve the liquid.

2. Place the wakame in a small bowl and fill with cool water for 10 seconds. Drain off the water, then cover with cool water and soak for 15 minutes. Lift out the wakame with your hands and chop coarsely.

3. In a Dutch oven or soup pot, bring 6 cups water, the reserved liquid from the skillet, the wakame, ginger, shoyu, and seared beef to a boil. Reduce the heat and simmer covered for 1 to 1½ hours, until the beef is very tender. To test for tenderness, remove a piece and pull it apart with a fork. It should pull apart easily.

4. Heat the remaining 1 tablespoon oil in the skillet and sauté the mushrooms and garlic until moisture is released from the mushrooms and they are just lightly browned. Add the cayenne and salt. Cook for 3 more minutes until the moisture has evaporated. Set aside and add to the beef mixture when the beef is tender. Simmer for 10 minutes, then stir in the scallions. Serve.

Variations

To make this a one-pot meal, add cooked grains or pasta to the soup bowls before ladling in the soup.

If you prefer serving smaller pieces of beef, remove the chunks from the pot with tongs prior to adding the mushrooms and garlic. Let them cool, then thinly slice them and return the slices to the pot.

# Salads

Arame, delicate and tender, has a unique mild flavor. This sea vegetable can be eaten without being cooked, so it is suitable for many quick dishes. This marinated arame is quick and easy to prepare. Sometimes I marinate the arame alone and leave it in the refrigerator to be added later to simple pasta dishes, lettuce salads, and grains.

Oversoaking arame will cause it to lose its delicate flavor. After 10 minutes, if you are not ready to use it, lift it from the soaking water and set it aside. If it dries out slightly on top, turn it over in the bowl and it will quickly rehydrate from the moisture on the bottom.

Avocado-Arame Guacamole

Makes 6 servings

½ cup loosely packed arame

2 teaspoons tamari

1 teaspoon brown rice vinegar (see box)

1 teaspoon pure maple syrup

2 ribs celery, cut in small dice

1 red bell pepper, seeded and cut in small dice

4 scallions, finely chopped

Juice of 2 limes

2 tablespoons extra virgin olive oil

½ teaspoon sea salt

½ cup cilantro, finely chopped

2 ripe avocados, peeled and cut in medium dice

1. Rinse the arame by placing it in a bowl and covering it with water. With your fingers, stir it for 5 seconds and drain. Cover it with fresh cool water and soak 10 minutes—not longer. Lift the arame out with your hands. Place it in a bowl with the tamari, vinegar, and maple syrup. Set aside to marinate.

2. Place the celery, bell pepper, scallions, lime juice, oil, salt, and cilantro in a bowl. Using a wooden spoon, mix well.

3. Gently toss the avocado in the lime mixture.

4. Stir in the marinated arame. Serve immediately.

> Brown rice vinegar is made from fermented brown rice. It is more delicate than other vinegars, with a less acidic and mellow quality that imposes less on other flavors. Most other vinegars will be too strong to use in place of it for the recipes in this book, but if you need a substitute, use apple cider vinegar, since it has a sweet-sour taste.

Arranging the salads individually, rather than mixing everything in one bowl, keeps the greens lightly dressed and fresher. The toasted smoked dulse maintains its crunch and smoky taste longer if added just before serving.

Goat cheese should remain in the refrigerator as close to serving time as possible so that it will hold its shape when sliced into rounds.

Smoked Dulse and Goat Cheese Salad

Makes 4 servings

½ cup tightly packed smoked dulse

3 cups mesclun greens, rinsed and dried

11-ounce log mild goat cheese, sliced into eighteen ¼-inch rounds

6 tablespoons walnut oil or extra virgin olive oil

4 teaspoons apple cider vinegar

4 teaspoons balsamic vinegar

1 cup toasted walnuts, coarsely chopped (see Note, page 64)

1. Heat a small skillet over a low flame for 30 seconds. Tear the dulse by hand into ¼- to ½-inch pieces. Drop into the skillet and heat for 5 minutes, or until the pieces turn brown, dry and crunchy. Stir several times with a wooden spoon.

2. Place the greens on individual serving plates. Form into a pyramid. Add 3 rounds of cheese to each plate, propping them around the greens.

3. Drizzle 1½ tablespoons oil, 1 teaspoon apple cider vinegar, and 1 teaspoon balsamic vinegar over each serving of greens and cheese.

4. Sprinkle 2 tablespoons toasted dulse over each serving of greens. Garnish with the chopped walnuts.

Variation

Rather than serving the cheese in rounds, gently break the rounds into ½-inch pieces and sprinkle on top of the salad greens before adding the dulse and walnuts.

Either West Coast wild nori or laver can be used. However, nori is a bit more tender and less salty. This salad, with a little heat from the ginger and hot sauce, is great with barbecued chicken, baked fish steaks, or grilled tofu.

Spiced Slaw

Makes 6 servings

½ cup kiri kombu, rinsed under cool running water for 15 seconds

½ cup wild nori (or laver), rinsed under cool running water for 15 seconds

½ small head red cabbage, shredded

½ small head Napa cabbage, shredded

1 small jícama, peeled and cut in thin, 2-inch strips

¼ red onion, minced

1 teaspoon sea salt

For the dressing

1 cup whole milk yogurt

2 tablespoons toasted sesame oil

2 tablespoons apple cider vinegar

3 tablespoons ginger juice

1½ tablespoons medium hot sauce

1. Bring 2 cups water to a boil, add the kombu and nori, and boil for 15 minutes. Drain through a strainer and rinse with cold water for 10 seconds. Coarsely chop the sea vegetables together. Set aside.

2. In a large salad bowl, mix the cabbages, jícama, onion, and salt. Work this mixture by hand, firmly rubbing the salt into the vegetables. In 5 minutes moisture will be drawn out of the vegetables and onto your hands. Add the chopped sea vegetables. Mix well.

3. Whisk together all the dressing ingredients in a separate bowl. Pour the dressing over the vegetables and toss well with two wooden spoons. Cover and refrigerate at least 1 hour to marinate. Stir once before serving.

Variation

Regular kombu can replace the kiri kombu, but it requires 10 minutes soaking time after its initial rinsing and before boiling.

Substituting sea palm for the anchovies gives the salad that familiar briny flavor. A bowl of hot pasta with red sauce is the ideal accompaniment.

Sea Vegetable Caesar Salad

Makes 4 servings

2 cups loosely packed sea palm
(see Note)

1 tablespoon plus 1 teaspoon
brown rice vinegar
(see box, page 51)

1 tablespoon plus 1 teaspoon tamari

4 cloves garlic, minced

For the dressing

½ cup extra virgin olive oil

2 tablespoons Dijon mustard

1 tablespoon lemon juice

2 teaspoons capers, coarsely chopped

¼ cup apple cider vinegar

½ cup grated Parmesan

1 head of romaine, washed, spun dry,
and cut into 2-inch strips

3 cups garlic croutons

1. Rinse the sea palm in a bowl under cool running water for 5 seconds. Fill the bowl with water to cover the sea palm completely. Soak for 1 hour. Lift the sea palm out with your hands and rinse in a strainer with cool, running water for 10 seconds. Place the sea palm in a bowl and add the brown rice vinegar, tamari, and garlic. Mix well. Marinate at room temperature for 2 hours. Lift the sea palm out of the marinade and set aside. Discard the marinade.

2. In a bowl mix the oil, mustard, lemon juice, capers, and apple cider vinegar. Whisk until creamy, about 1 minute. Add the Parmesan and whisk again briefly.

3. In a serving bowl toss the romaine, half of the sea palm, the dressing, and half of the croutons. Make sure everything is coated with dressing. Garnish with the rest of the sea palm and the croutons. Serve immediately.

Note: Jump-start this salad by preparing the sea palm the night before. It can withstand long soaking. Soak it overnight in the refrigerator. In the morning, drain and rinse it, prepare the marinade, and let the sea palm sit in the refrigerator during the day. In the evening, prepare the lettuce and dressing. The sea palm will be slightly softer in texture but will have a stronger garlic flavor.

Wild nori, not processed like sheet or "sushi" nori, has an amazing crunchy texture that holds up through rinsing, soaking, and cooking and is also less sweet than sheet nori. Once soaked, wild nori turns a translucent purplish blue. The combination of peas and nori reminds me of the way wild nori clings to rocks in the sea. This is a flavorful warm-weather salad with fresh herbs, a vibrant vinegar, and sundried tomatoes.

Umeboshi vinegar, not a true vinegar, is the brine that surrounds pickled Japanese plums. It has a salty and sour flavor and is much more concentrated than other vinegars.

Wild Nori in Black-Eyed Peas

Makes 4 servings

5 small sundried tomatoes

1 cup black-eyed peas,
soaked in water for 2 hours

½ cup firmly packed wild nori

1 teaspoon tamari

¼ cup extra virgin olive oil

1 tablespoon brown rice vinegar
(see box, page 51)

1 teaspoon umeboshi vinegar

2 teaspoons Dijon mustard

½ tablespoon pure maple syrup

½ teaspoon sea salt

3 tablespoons chopped chives

3 tablespoons minced parsley

3 tablespoons chopped cilantro

1. Cover the tomatoes with 1½ cups boiling water and soak for 15 minutes, until they have completely softened. Pour off the water and finely chop the tomatoes.

2. Drain the peas and rinse with cold water. Place them in a pot with 4 cups water and bring to a boil. Lower the flame and simmer 20 minutes, until tender but not falling apart. Drain off the cooking liquid. Set aside in a large bowl and add the tomatoes.

3. Boil the wild nori and tamari uncovered in 1 cup water for 15 minutes, or until all the liquid evaporates. Cool, finely chop, and add to the peas.

4. Whisk together the olive oil, vinegars, mustard, maple syrup, and salt. Add the chives, parsley, and cilantro. Add the mixture to the peas and stir well. Serve chilled or at room temperature.

Soba are thin Japanese buckwheat noodles. Arame resembles delicate black pasta. When the arame and soba are intertwined it's like eating two kinds of noodles. Each bite has a hot and sweet flavor.

The dressing, noodles, and arame can be prepared ahead of time. Assemble just before serving.

Soba Salad

Makes 4 servings

8-ounce package soba noodles

½ cup lightly packed arame

2 teaspoons tamari

½ cup toasted sesame oil

3 tablespoons brown rice vinegar (see box, page 51)

2 tablespoons pure maple syrup

1 tablespoon Dijon mustard

2 teaspoons sea salt

4 cups bean sprouts, rinsed and drained

6 scallions, thinly sliced on the diagonal

1. In a large pot, boil 3 quarts of water. Add the noodles and cook until the noodles are the same color inside and outside, 5 to 7 minutes. Drain and rinse under warm water and place in a large serving bowl.

2. Rinse the arame in a bowl of cool water for 5 seconds and drain. Cover with water and soak for 7 minutes. Lift the arame out of the water with your hands and place it in a small bowl. Add the tamari and stir well to coat the arame. Add to the noodles, mixing well with two large wooden spoons.

3. Whisk together in a small bowl the oil, vinegar, maple syrup, mustard, and salt. Pour the dressing over the noodles, mixing well again. Add the sprouts and scallions and give the mixture a quick toss before serving.

Variations

Cooked small shrimp or steamed tofu may be added for a more robust salad.

Sea vegetables that have been soaked but not cooked more closely resemble those in their natural state. This mixture of sea vegetables—mild and strong—offers shades of green and varying textures in a vinegar dressing. For the adventurous seaweed lover!

Crunch 'n' Brine Salad

Makes 6 servings

1 cup loosely packed wakame

½ cup loosely packed kiri kombu

½ cup loosely packed sea palm

2 tablespoons tamari

6 tablespoons brown rice vinegar (see box, page 51)

¼ cup pure maple syrup

1 tablespoon plus 1 teaspoon umeboshi vinegar

1. In a large bowl, rinse the sea vegetables twice with cool water for 10 seconds and drain well. Set aside in a large bowl.

2. Bring 6 cups of water and the tamari to a boil. Pour over the sea vegetables and let sit for 10 minutes. Drain.

3. Whisk together the vinegars and maple syrup. Mix well with the sea vegetables. Cover and refrigerate for 30 minutes.

Note: This is delicious served inside radicchio leaves or dressed with Smoked Dulse and Basil Infusion (see page 103).

Chicken salad is enhanced in texture by sea palm, which also adds a deep green color to this salad, dressed with a sweet, creamy cashew butter and yogurt dressing. It's a great filling for pita or served over red leaf or Bibb lettuce.

Sea Palm Chicken Salad with Roasted Garlic

Makes 6 servings

2 bulbs garlic
1 tablespoon extra virgin olive oil
¾ cup loosely packed sea palm
3 teaspoons extra virgin olive oil
Dash of black pepper
½ teaspoon sea salt
4 boneless, skinless chicken breasts

For the dressing

¼ cup cashew butter,
at room temperature
1 cup whole milk yogurt
2 teaspoons sea salt
Dash of black pepper

2 ribs celery, minced
2 carrots, shredded
2 heads of Bibb lettuce

1. Preheat the oven to 375°F. Cut off the top third of the garlic and drizzle the olive oil on top. Wrap in foil and bake for 45 minutes until the cloves are tender. They should be a deep golden brown. A paring knife should pierce them easily. Set aside until cool. Squeeze the cloves out of their skin and set aside in a bowl.

2. Rinse the sea palm for 5 seconds in a bowl of cool water. Drain. Cover with water and soak for 10 minutes. Lift out with your hands and set aside.

3. In a Dutch oven or medium soup pot, bring 6 cups of water, the sea palm, pepper, and salt to a boil. Add the chicken, return to a boil, then lower the heat and simmer for 7 to 10 minutes, or until there is no pink visible on the chicken. Remove the chicken and sea palm with a slotted spoon. Let cool for 15 minutes in a bowl.

4. In a small bowl, combine the roasted cloves of garlic, the cashew butter, yogurt, salt, and pepper, using a fork to blend the ingredients well. Set aside.

5. Place the celery and carrots in a large bowl. Tear the chicken and sea palm into bite-size pieces by hand and add to the bowl. Add the dressing and mix well.

6. To serve the salad, make a small cup with 3 Bibb leaves and place 1 cup of salad in the center. Crackers may be placed around the lettuce.

A refreshing, citrus-salty flavor. The vermilion blood orange slices peek out from among the long black strands of hijiki. Frisée makes a gentle nest to hold the salad.

If pineapple juice is not available, substitute 1½ cups of fresh orange juice. Navel oranges can be substituted for blood oranges.

Citrus Hijiki with Roasted Nuts

Makes 4 servings

½ cup hijiki

1 cup unsweetened pineapple juice

½ cup fresh orange juice

¼ teaspoon sea salt

1½ tablespoons walnut oil
plus some for drizzling

2 teaspoons balsamic vinegar

3 blood oranges, separated into pieces
without membranes

2 tablespoons chopped fresh dill

1 bunch frisée

½ cup toasted walnuts,
coarsely chopped (see Note)

1. Rinse the hijiki in a bowl of cool water for 15 seconds. Drain. Soak in the bowl with water to cover for 30 minutes. The hijiki will soak up most of the water. Lift the hijiki out of the water with your hands and squeeze out any remaining water. Discard the soaking water.

2. Place the hijiki, pineapple juice, orange juice, and salt in a pot. Bring to a boil, then reduce the heat and simmer until the juice is evaporated, 20 to 30 minutes.

3. Transfer the cooked hijiki to a serving bowl. Add the oil and vinegar, mixing well. Add the orange pieces and dill, tossing lightly to combine.

4. Place small sections of the frisée on each salad plate and lightly drizzle with walnut oil. Place ¾ cup of the hijiki salad in the center of each plate. Garnish with the walnuts and serve.

Note: To toast walnuts: Preheat the oven to 325°F. Spread the walnuts on a baking sheet and bake for 5 to 10 minutes, or until golden. Avoid over-toasting as they will taste bitter.

The complementary flavors of the three sea vegetables in this salad combine for a unique blend of flavor and a chewy texture. The sea vegetables, left whole, give each bite of this salad ribbon-like strands, thickly coated with sesame seeds. The taste is at once sweet, salty, sour, and nutty.

Jungle Green Salad with Seeds

Makes 6 servings

1 cup loosely packed kiri kombu

½ cup loosely packed arame

1 cup loosely packed sea palm

¼ cup tamari

2 tablespoons mirin

1 tablespoon pure maple syrup

¼ cup walnut oil

2 tablespoons apple cider vinegar

1 cup brown sesame seeds, toasted

1 cup unsalted roasted peanuts, lightly crushed

1. Rinse the kiri kombu, arame, and sea palm together in a bowl of cool water for 10 seconds. Drain. Repeat.

2. In a small pot, bring 4 cups water, the kombu, arame, sea palm, tamari, mirin, and maple syrup to a boil and boil for 15 minutes, uncovered.

3. Drain the sea vegetables in a colander and place in a serving bowl. Pour the oil and vinegar over the warm sea vegetables and toss well. Add all the sesame seeds and peanuts and toss thoroughly again. Serve warm.

Notes: Japanese or West Coast kombu can be substituted for kiri kombu. After boiling it with the other sea vegetables, let it cool and cut it into long thin strands. Kiri kombu comes in long narrow strands.

To crush the peanuts, put them in a plastic bag and lightly pound them with a meat tenderizer or small rolling pin.

# Entrees

This entree, richly flavored with Kalamata olives and garlic, is great served over lightly oiled fettuccine. The baby artichoke and arame melt in your mouth, and the deep colors and various textures create a hearty meal.

Sweet Arame over Baby Artichokes

Makes 4 servings

8 baby artichokes
(4 artichoke halves in each serving)
Juice of ½ lemon
1 cup loosely packed arame
1 cup extra virgin olive oil
10 cloves garlic, chopped
8 Kalamata olives, pitted and chopped
1 tablespoon tamari
2 teaspoons sea salt
Black pepper to taste
1 pound fettuccine or other pasta

1. Trim the artichokes and peel the stems. Remove the outer leaves and cut each artichoke in half lengthwise. Place them, until needed, in enough water to cover and add the lemon juice to avoid discoloration.

2. Rinse the arame in cool water for 5 seconds, then cover with cool water and soak for 10 minutes. Lift the arame out of the water with your hands and chop coarsely.

3. Heat the oil in a large, heavy skillet over medium heat for 3 to 5 minutes, or until the oil starts to move slightly. Remove the artichokes from the water and wipe off excess water. Place cut side down in the hot oil to fry. The oil should half cover the artichokes. Cover the skillet and continue cooking over medium heat for 15 minutes, or until they become light olive green and tender. When they are tender, the tip of a sharp knife should go in easily.

4. Place the garlic in the skillet on top of the artichokes and then layer the arame over the garlic. Cook for 10 minutes, until the garlic is fragrant. Drain off any excess oil and discard. Return the skillet to low heat for 10 minutes, add the olives, tamari, and salt. Gently toss to mix. Serve over fettuccine or your favorite pasta.

The sweet essence of nori combined with fresh thyme and lemon season the fish. As the fish swells slightly as it cooks, the nori wrap tightens, forming an attractive black-green blanket. Each fillet makes a 3-inch-square bundle.

Serve with white rice and sautéed red cabbage.

Nori-Wrapped Sole

Makes 4 servings

2½ **pounds lemon sole fillets, cut into 3-inch-square pieces**

¼ **cup lemon juice**

¾ **tablespoon chopped fresh thyme**

1 **teaspoon sea salt**

9 **sheets toasted nori, cut into 3-inch-wide strips (cut the entire length of the sheet on the side with the vertical lines)**

2 **tablespoons extra virgin olive oil**

1 **tablespoon butter**

4 **lemon wedges**

1. Place the fillet squares side by side in a long baking pan. Pour the lemon juice on top and sprinkle with the thyme and the salt. Marinate for 15 minutes.

2. Place a strip of nori on a cutting board. Put a fish square on the end of the nori closest to you. Quickly roll up the fish in the nori until you reach the end of the strip. Set the roll seam side down on a large plate. Repeat for each piece of fish.

3. Heat the oil and butter on low heat for 20 seconds. Put 7 or 8 pieces of fish in the oil, seam side down. (Placing them seam side down helps the nori stick and form a tight seal.) Cook gently on low heat for 5 minutes, until the nori on the bottom is dark green–black and crispy. Flip it over with a spatula. Cover the skillet for 3 minutes to finish the cooking. The fish bundles will puff up slightly and the nori will look taut. Drain briefly on paper towels. Serve with a light sprinkle of sea salt and a lemon wedge.

Quick cooking of arame brings the sweet and sour flavors together and welcomes all seasonings. Serve with any grain or pasta.

Arrowroot is a powdered starch from the root of a tropical plant. I use it instead of cornstarch. You can find it in most supermarkets in the baking section.

Sweet-and-Sour Tofu Stir-Fry

Makes 4 servings

¾ cup lightly packed arame

For the sauce

1 cup fresh orange juice

2 tablespoons tamari

2 tablespoons apple cider vinegar

2 tablespoons pure maple syrup

¼ teaspoon red pepper flakes

3 cloves garlic, minced

2 tablespoons arrowroot

2 tablespoons toasted sesame oil

1 red onion, cut into 1-inch pieces

1½ pounds extra firm tofu, drained and cut into ½-inch cubes

2 carrots, cut into 2-inch matchsticks

¼ head broccoli, cut into 2-inch florets

12 shiitakes, stems removed, sliced in half

1½ cups pineapple chunks

1½ cups raw cashews, coarsely chopped

1. Rinse the arame for 5 seconds with cool water. Cover with fresh water and soak for 7 minutes. Lift it out with your hands, chop coarsely, and set aside.

2. In a bowl, whisk together the orange juice, tamari, vinegar, maple syrup, pepper flakes, and garlic. Add the arrowroot, mixing well. Set aside.

3. Heat the oil in a wok or large, heavy skillet over medium-high heat for 20 seconds. Add the onion and toss with two large wooden spoons or heatproof spatulas for 30 seconds, until the onion is wilted. Add the tofu and cook for 3 minutes until golden. Add the carrots and broccoli, tossing for 5 minutes until the broccoli is bright green. Add the arame, shiitakes, and pineapple, and cook for 2 to 3 minutes until the shiitakes are lightly browned and slightly wilted. Add the sauce, stirring quickly for about 2 minutes, until it loses its slightly creamy color and thickens. Add the cashews and cook for 1 minute more. Serve hot.

The three marinated sea vegetables used in this dish add a variety of textures, mild sea flavors, and color to the shrimp. The herbs marry the gifts of the sea, creating a sumptuous, festive dish. It is spicy, with lots of garlic and chili flavors in each mouthful. Serve over rice. Great for a buffet—you can triple the recipe.

Mariscal with Shrimp

Makes 4 servings

1 cup loosely packed arame

1 cup loosely packed ito wakame

8-inch strip kombu

4 cloves garlic, minced

½ cup minced red onion

2 jalapeño chiles,
seeded and finely chopped

2 tablespoons tamari

4 minced scallions

¼ cup minced cilantro

¼ cup minced flat-leaf parsley

20 jumbo shrimp, cooked and halved

¾ cup extra virgin olive oil

½ cup lemon juice

Sea salt and black pepper to taste

4 lemon slices

1. Rinse the arame in a bowl under cool running water for 5 seconds. Drain. Soak in cool water to cover for 10 minutes. Lift it out with your hands. Chop coarsely and set aside. Rinse the wakame under cool running water for 5 seconds. Soak in water to cover for 20 minutes. Lift it out with your hands. Chop coarsely. Rinse the kombu under cool running water for 5 seconds. Boil 5 minutes in 2 cups of water. Lift it out with tongs and let cool. Slice very thin crosswise.

2. In a bowl, combine the arame, wakame, kombu, garlic, onion, jalapeño, tamari, and ¼ cup water. Stir to mix well. Let sit for 30 minutes at room temperature to marinate the sea vegetables.

3. Add the scallions, cilantro, parsley, and shrimp to the marinating mixture and toss lightly. Drizzle the oil and lemon juice over the mixture and toss again. Add salt and pepper to taste and serve immediately. Garnish with the lemon slices.

Kombumaki is a technique of Japanese cooking in which seaweed is tied around food to secure it prior to cooking. The tied food is then poached in water or stock. In this recipe, long strands of kiri kombu are tied around chicken pieces, providing flavor to the chicken and broth. Yukon gold potatoes are a creamy and delicious addition.

When I feel a cold coming on, this is the dish I crave. It's warming, easy to digest, and comforting.

Stir in 2 cups of chopped spinach, Swiss chard, or turnip greens during the last 5 minutes of cooking for an additional flavor boost.

Chicken Kombumaki

Makes 6 servings

8 sprigs thyme

10 sprigs flat-leaf parsley plus ½ cup chopped, for garnish

2 onions, quartered

2 carrots, cut into 3-inch lengths

3 Yukon gold potatoes, peeled and cut into 2-inch pieces

1 rib celery, cut into 3-inch lengths

1 cup kiri kombu

3 boneless, skinless chicken breasts

2 teaspoons sea salt

1 tablespoon butter

1. Tie the thyme and parsley together with a 5-inch piece of cooking twine, making a knot. Bring the onions, carrots, potatoes, celery, thyme, parsley, and 2 cups water to a boil. Lower the heat and simmer for 30 minutes. Remove the parsley and thyme with tongs and discard.

2. Rinse the kombu twice in a bowl of cool water. Cover with water and soak for 10 minutes. Lift it out with your hands and set aside.

3. Cut the chicken breasts crosswise into ½-inch strips. Tie a strip of kombu around the center of each chicken strip and make a knot. Be careful not to pull the strips too tightly as you knot them, so they don't tear.

4. Add the salt, butter, and chicken/kombu pieces to the vegetables and bring to a boil. Reduce the heat and simmer for 15 minutes, or until there is no pink remaining in the chicken. Serve over a combination of wild rice and brown basmati rice, garnished with the chopped parsley.

This is similar to the Russian dish prepared with beef. The wakame softens and seasons the chicken while becoming creamy in the sour cream. The garlic-dulse flakes, a condiment available at health food stores, spices up the stroganoff.

Serve over noodles or your favorite grain.

Chicken Stroganoff

Makes 4 servings

¼ cup lightly packed ito wakame

4 boneless, skinless chicken breasts

¼ cup extra virgin olive oil

1 large onion, thinly sliced

4 cups button mushrooms, thinly sliced

5 cloves garlic, minced

Sea salt and black pepper to taste

1½ cups sour cream

¼ cup minced flat-leaf parsley

2 teaspoons garlic-dulse flakes

1. In a small bowl, rinse the wakame with cool water for 10 seconds. Cover with water and soak for 5 minutes. Lift it out with your hands and set aside.

2. Place each chicken breast between two sheets of plastic wrap and pound to a thickness of ½ inch. Cut the fillets into 1-inch diagonal strips.

3. Heat 1 tablespoon of the oil in a large skillet on a low flame. Cook the onion slowly until soft and transparent. Add the mushrooms and cook until golden brown. Stir in the garlic and wakame and continue cooking for 10 minutes until the wakame has darkened and the garlic has permeated the other ingredients. Remove from the heat and set aside in a bowl.

4. Pour the remaining oil into the skillet and increase the heat to medium. Fry the chicken in small batches for 3 to 4 minutes until opaque, with no pink visible.

5. Put all of the chicken and the onion and mushroom mixture into the skillet. Season with salt and pepper and stir in the sour cream. Slowly bring to a boil, lower the heat, and simmer for 5 minutes. Turn off the heat and transfer the stroganoff to a serving platter. Garnish with the parsley and and the garlic-dulse flakes.

Although kombu is a thick and tough sea vegetable, it imparts a delicate flavor to the fish while preventing it from sticking to the pan. The edges of the kombu become crispy and salty. The salmon served with kombu attached is like a gift package.

Accompany with a romaine salad, dressed with a light vinaigrette dressing.

Roasted Salmon Steaks with Kombu

Makes 4 servings

Four 6-inch strips kombu

1 tablespoon plus 1 teaspoon extra virgin olive oil

1 tablespoon plus 1 teaspoon butter

Four 1½ inch thick salmon steaks

1 teaspoon tamari

1 red onion, minced

4 cloves garlic, minced

½ teaspoon sea salt

Dash of black pepper

½ cup chopped cilantro

4 lemon wedges

1. Preheat the oven to 350°F.

2. Rinse the kombu strips in cold water for 5 seconds. Place in a bowl with fresh cool water for 5 minutes. Lift the kombu out with your hands and set aside.

3. Grease a long baking sheet with the 1 teaspoon oil and the l teaspoon butter. Line the baking sheet with the kombu strips, leaving a 4-inch space between each one. Place the salmon steaks on top of the kombu, making sure the salmon is resting only on the kombu. If your strips of kombu are narrow, add a second piece next to each one. Drizzle the tamari over the salmon. Set aside.

4. Heat the 1 tablespoon of olive oil and the 1 tablespoon of butter in a skillet over medium heat, then add the onion and garlic, cooking for 2 minutes until the onion is transparent and the garlic is fragrant. Add the salt, pepper, and cilantro and remove from the heat after only a minute, just long enough for the cilantro to wilt. Cover the surface of each salmon steak with a thin layer of the onion-herb mixture. Cover with foil and bake for 15 minutes. Uncover and continue cooking for 15 to 20 minutes or until the fish is completely opaque. Remove the fish from the baking sheet with a spatula, making sure each steak has kombu attached. Garnish with the lemon wedges.

"Ageh" means pan- or deep-fried in Japanese. The silky texture of the sea palm, pasta, and coconut milk combine with the fried tofu for a rich, creamy, earth-colored duo.

Serve with a side of steamed carrots and kale.

Age Tofu in Sea Palm

Makes 4 servings

1 pound extra firm tofu

½ cup sea palm

1½ cups fusilli or rotini

¼ cup plus 1 tablespoon coconut oil or canola oil

1 red onion, thinly sliced

½ pound cremini mushrooms, quartered

1 cup coconut milk

1¼ teaspoons sea salt

½ cup chopped flat-leaf parsley

1. Place the tofu in a shallow bowl. Place a weighted plate on top of the tofu. This will press the excess water out of the tofu, allowing it to fry better. Press for 30 minutes, then drain off the excess water. The tofu will be denser and less pliable. Cut it into fourteen ½-inch-thick pieces.

2. Rinse the sea palm quickly in cool water for about 5 seconds. Then cover with cool water and soak for 15 minutes. Lift out with your hands and set aside.

3. Bring 4 cups of water to a boil. Add the pasta and cook for 12 minutes until al dente. Drain and set aside.

4. Heat the ¼ cup oil in a large skillet over medium heat for 45 seconds, or until the oil makes small spirals. Add the pressed tofu slabs. Fry until golden brown, 5 to 7 minutes on each side. Using a spatula, remove the tofu and drain on paper towels. Set aside. When cool enough to handle, cut the tofu slabs into ¼-inch strips.

5. In a 5-inch-deep pot, heat the 1 tablespoon oil over medium heat. Add the onion and mushrooms and cook for 5 minutes until the mushrooms release moisture and are lightly browned. Add the sea palm and stir to avoid sticking. Cook for 2 minutes. Pour the coconut milk and ½ cup water into the pot, lower the heat to a simmer, add the tofu strips, cover, and cook for 5 minutes. Add the cooked pasta and salt. Simmer 10 minutes, until the entire mixture is thick and creamy. Stir in the parsley and remove from the heat. Serve immediately.

These tasty patties are made with fresh rather than canned salmon and dulse. Serve them as an entree with a creamy sauce on top or on the side. A quick sauce may be made with equal amounts of Dijon mustard and mayonnaise, whisked together. A baby arugula or wilted spinach salad completes these crowd pleasers.

Salmon Cakes

Makes 20 half-dollar-size cakes or 4 servings

1-pound salmon fillet

Juice of 1 lemon

¼ cup tightly packed smoked dulse

⅓ cup minced flat-leaf parsley

¼ cup chopped dill

4 scallions, minced

½ cup extra virgin olive oil

2 tablespoons Dijon mustard

¼ teaspoon sea salt

2 eggs, lightly beaten

1 cup unseasoned bread crumbs

1. Simmer the salmon, skin side down, in ½ inch water in a covered skillet for 10 minutes, or until the salmon is no longer transparent pink on the inside. With a spatula, remove the salmon from the pan and let cool. Remove the skin and any bones.

2. Put the salmon in a bowl, add the lemon juice, and, with a fork, crumble the salmon well.

3. Moisten the dulse by putting it in your hand, making a loose fist, and holding it under cool running water for 5 seconds. It will soften quickly. Tear it into small pieces and add to the crumbled salmon. Add the parsley, dill, and scallions to the salmon and stir well. Add 1 tablespoon of the olive oil, the mustard, salt, and eggs and mix well. Gently stir in the bread crumbs and form the mixture into 4-inch patties. Cover and refrigerate 1 hour.

4. In a medium skillet, heat the remaining olive oil. Fry the cakes on each side until golden. Drain well on paper towels.

Note: Salmon cakes can be kept warm in a 200°F oven for 20 to 30 minutes.

In this dish, fish is wrapped in parchment paper. Alaria adds a light saltiness to oven-steamed fish, sweet vegetables, and herbs, becoming as tender as the fish. The parchment pouches always look inviting to open.

If you prefer to use a fish like salmon or tuna that cooks longer or is oilier than flounder, substitute kombu for the alaria. You will need four sheets of parchment paper to make this dish.

Fish en Papillote

Makes 4 servings

Four 6-inch strips alaria

1 tablespoon butter

1 tablespoon extra virgin olive oil plus some for the parchment paper

1 carrot, cut into 3-inch matchsticks

1 zucchini, cut into 3-inch matchsticks

1 red onion, coarsely minced

2 leeks, cut into 3-inch matchsticks

Four 6-ounce flounder fillets or fish of your choice

¼ teaspoon sea salt

Dash of black pepper

¼ cup dry white wine

¼ cup chopped dill

4 lemon slices

1. Preheat the oven to 375°F.

2. Rinse the alaria for 5 seconds under cool water, then cover and soak for 10 minutes. Lift out of the soaking water with your hands and set aside.

3. In a skillet over medium-high heat, combine the butter and the 1 tablespoon oil. Add the carrots, zucchini, onion, and leeks and cook, stirring frequently, for 5 minutes or until the vegetables are tender. Set aside.

4. Fold 4 sheets of parchment paper, 12 by 18 inches each, in half and cut out a large half heart shape in the fold. Open the cutouts into full hearts and brush each with oil. Place a strip of alaria on one half of each heart-shaped piece and place a fillet on top of it. Sprinkle the fillets with salt and pepper. Divide the vegetable mixture equally among the four papers, place on top of the fish, drizzle with the wine, and sprinkle with the dill. Top with a slice of lemon.

5. Fold the opposite side of the heart-shaped paper over the fish. Starting at the top, roll the edges in, toward you, forming a sealed pouch, all the way to the bottom. The pouches should be shaped like half hearts and be full in the center. Place the pouches on an ungreased baking sheet and bake for 15 to 20 minutes. The parchment will be light brown and puff up when the fish is done. Serve at once with basmati rice and a lightly dressed fresh green salad.

Making tempura is a lot of fun, and sea vegetables have a salty taste that makes them wonderful candidates for deep-frying. Any sea vegetable can be used for tempura. When fried just right, tempura is crispy, rich, and satisfying. Experiment to discover your favorites or mix them.

Organization is essential. Eating tempura fresh and hot is the only way to enjoy it! Have the food, utensils, and paper towels ready. Be sure to have separate tongs or chopsticks for putting the arame into the batter and then for lifting it out of the hot oil to be drained.

Serve with rice and a fresh salad and provide each person with a tablespoon of grated raw daikon with a splash of shoyu to help digest the oil. Daikon can be purchased in Asian markets.

Sea Vegetable Tempura

Makes 4 servings

For the batter

2 cups whole wheat pastry flour
1 teaspoon garlic powder
2 teaspoons arrowroot
½ cup beer

2 cups loosely packed arame
2 tablespoons toasted sesame oil
4 shallots, thinly sliced
2 carrots, cut into 2-inch matchsticks
¼ cup shoyu
4 cups safflower or sunflower oil or canola oil

For the dipping sauce

¼ cup shoyu
2 tablespoons lemon juice
1 tablespoon ginger juice

1. Whisk the flour, garlic powder, and arrowroot together in a bowl. Stirring well, add 1 cup water and the beer, creating a medium-thick batter. Cover and refrigerate for 30 to 40 minutes. The batter will thicken as it chills.

2. Rinse the arame in cool water for 5 seconds, cover with water, and soak for 10 minutes. Lift it out with your hands and set aside.

3. Heat the sesame oil in a skillet over medium heat for 10 seconds and add the shallots. Sauté until golden brown, about 5 minutes. Add the arame, 2 cups of water, and 2 tablespoons of the shoyu. Bring to a boil, then lower the heat and simmer for 15 minutes, then add the carrots and cook until almost all the liquid has evaporated, 5 to 10 minutes. Add the remaining 2 tablespoons shoyu and cook for 2 to 3 minutes more over medium heat. Transfer to a bowl and let the mixture cool.

4. Heat the oil in a wok over medium heat. To test to see if the oil is hot enough, drop in a small amount of batter. It should sink to the bottom, then come right back to the surface. If the oil smokes, it is too hot. Using tongs or wooden chopsticks, pick up half-dollar-size portions of the arame mixture and drop them into the chilled batter. Quickly lift them out and put them into the hot oil. Deep-fry on each side until golden, about 2 minutes. Fry only 5 or 6 pieces at a time. This way the oil will stay hot. Remove each piece separately and place on paper towels to drain. Serve immediately with the dipping sauce.

5. In a small mixing bowl, combine the dipping sauce ingredients and ½ cup water. Pour ¼ cup of this mixture into each of 4 dipping bowls.

Tempeh is a staple in Indonesia. Made with a base of fermented yellow soybeans, it is versatile in cooking and popular in vegetarian diets as a protein source. There are a variety of tempeh flavors on the market. It is sold as a thick, dense square or rectangle.

With hijiki's strong, salty flavor setting off the tempeh, this dish is one of my favorites when the weather starts getting chilly! Black strands of hijiki drape around tempeh cubes, and strands of bright orange carrot and green leek add appetizing color.

A tip on deep-frying tempeh: use an oil that has no flavor. Sunflower, safflower, and canola oils are fine, as they can be heated high without smoking and burning. When heating oil for deep-frying, use a heavy pot or wok to make sure the oil is warmed evenly and maintains a stable temperature while food is frying. Test to see if the oil is hot enough for frying by dropping in a tiny piece of tempeh. If it sinks to the bottom for several seconds and comes back to the top, the oil is ready. If it sits on the bottom, the oil is not hot enough. If the tempeh barely drops to the bottom and quickly shoots back to the top, the oil is too hot. In that case, lower the heat, wait, and test again.

Serve with steamed vegetables and a side of couscous. Deep-fried foods should be eaten at once.

Hijiki with Deep-Fried Tempeh

Makes 4 servings

1 cup dried hijiki

8-ounce package soy tempeh, cut into 1-inch cubes

3 tablespoons shoyu

3 cups canola oil

2 tablespoons toasted sesame oil

1 onion, minced

4 cups apple juice

2 carrots, cut into 3-inch matchsticks

2 leeks, white and green parts, thoroughly washed, cut into 3-inch diagonals

1. Rinse the hijiki under cool running water. Cover with water and soak for 20 minutes. Lift it out with your hands and squeeze out the excess water. Chop into coarse pieces.

2. Place the tempeh cubes in a bowl. Add 1¼ cups water and 1 tablespoon of the shoyu and mix well. Let sit for 45 minutes. Drain the tempeh and place on a paper towel–lined plate to absorb any moisture. Set aside.

3. Heat the canola oil in a skillet for deep-frying. Put in half the tempeh and deep-fry until golden brown, about 5 minutes. Remove to a paper towel–lined plate to drain. Repeat with the rest of the tempeh.

4. In a large skillet, heat the sesame oil and sauté the onion until golden, about 10 minutes. Add the hijiki and apple juice. Cover and bring to a boil. Reduce to a simmer and cook for 20 to 30 minutes, or until half the liquid has evaporated.

5. Add the carrots, fried tempeh, leeks, and the remaining 2 tablespoons shoyu. Cook for 15 to 20 minutes more, or until the liquid has evaporated.

Side Dishes

The sweet sea flavor of arame along with lots of lemon makes this vegetable braise taste of spring.

Lemony Spring Vegetables

Makes 4 servings

½ cup lightly packed arame

1 tablespoon extra virgin olive oil

2 spring onions,
white and green parts, thinly sliced

Juice of 2 large lemons

2½ pounds baby spinach

¼ pound fresh peas, shelled

½ teaspoon sea salt

4 lemon slices

1. Rinse the arame in cool water for 5 seconds, then cover with cool water and soak for 10 minutes. Lift the arame out with your hands and set aside.

2. Heat the oil in a skillet over low heat for 15 seconds, then put in the white onion part. Sauté for 5 minutes until transparent.

3. Stir in the arame, lemon juice, and 1 cup water. Put the spinach and green onion in the pan, but do not stir. Cover. Bring to a boil, then lower the heat and simmer for 3 to 5 minutes, or until the spinach is wilted. Add the peas and salt. Cook uncovered for 2 minutes more, or until most of the liquid has evaporated. Transfer to a serving platter; garnish with the lemon slices.

When you want more flavor than that of steamed Brussels sprouts alone, this vinaigrette-dressed vegetable dish, with earthy, smoky dulse, is perfect.

Brussels Sprouts with Smoked Dulse and Water Chestnuts

Makes 4 servings

1 pint Brussels sprouts, trimmed, outer leaves removed, halved lengthwise

5-ounce can water chestnuts, drained, rinsed, thinly sliced

¼ cup coarsely chopped flat-leaf parsley

3 tablespoons extra virgin olive oil

1 tablespoon brown rice vinegar (see box, page 51)

1 teaspoon sea salt

¼ cup chopped chives

1½ tablespoons smoked dulse flakes

1. Put a steamer basket into a pot, add enough water to barely cover the bottom of the steamer, and put in the Brussels sprouts.

2. Bring the water to a boil over medium heat and steam for 7 minutes, or until the sprouts are tender when pierced by a fork and light green in color. Wearing a mitt, remove the steamer basket. Set aside.

3. In a bowl, toss the chestnuts with the parsley and add the sprouts. Drizzle the oil, vinegar, and salt over the vegetables, then add the chives and dulse flakes. Toss to mix well. Transfer to a serving dish.

Variation

Cabbage is delicious prepared this way. Use half a small green cabbage. Cut it into 2-inch chunks and steam it. You can substitute 4 scallions for the parsley and chives.

When dried, grapestone is chewy in texture and red in color, but when cooked with coconut milk it becomes creamy and brown. Use as a topping for pasta or as a side dish.

Creamy Grapestone in Coconut Milk

Makes 4 servings

2 cups grapestone
1 tablespoon butter or coconut oil
1 large onion, coarsely chopped
½ teaspoon sea salt
2 tablespoons coconut milk

1. Rinse the grapestone in a bowl with cool water for 15 seconds, drain, and repeat. Cover with cold water and soak for an hour. Lift the grapestone from the water with your hands, gently squeeze out excess water, and set aside.

2. Heat a skillet over medium heat. Add the butter and onion and sauté for 2 minutes until the onion is transparent. Add the grapestone and salt and cook for 3 minutes, or until it turns brown.

3. Add 1½ cups water and cook for 10 minutes, uncovered. Add the coconut milk and simmer, stirring frequently, for 5 to 10 minutes until the consistency is creamy. Serve immediately.

The key to success here is to avoid overcooking. The kale should be cut into small pieces and cooked just until it is vibrant green, not dark green. The shiitakes are delicate, and quick cooking makes them tender and delicious. This is a savory, richly textured mushroom and green vegetable dish with garlic.

If fresh shiitakes are unavailable, substitute a combination of cremini and button mushrooms, but don't use dried shiitakes for this dish, since they are tougher and require longer cooking. Serve with grilled chicken or steak.

Seared Shiitakes

Makes 6 servings

1 bunch kale, cut into bite-size pieces

2 tablespoons extra virgin olive oil

½ pound shiitakes,
stems removed, thinly sliced

4 cloves garlic, minced

2 tablespoons tamari

3 sheets toasted nori,
torn into 1-inch pieces

1. Cook the kale in 2 quarts boiling water until bright green, about 4 minutes. Drain and set aside.

2. Heat the oil in a skillet over medium heat. Add the shiitakes and sauté, stirring frequently, until soft and lightly browned on the edges, about 3 minutes. Add the garlic. Mix well. Add the boiled kale and combine all the ingredients well.

3. Pour the tamari over the mixture, stir in the nori, and remove from the heat after any moisture has evaporated, about 3 minutes.

From stove to table in less than 5 minutes, this vegetable dish is perfect for a midweek family dinner. Serve with rice and another stir-fried dish.

Hijiki Snow Peas

Makes 4 servings

¼ **cup hijiki**

2 **teaspoons butter**

½ **pound snow peas**

2 **cloves garlic,
minced or thinly sliced**

½ **teaspoon sea salt**

1. Rinse the hijiki in a bowl with cool water for 10 seconds. Drain. Add 2 cups fresh water. Soak for 30 minutes. Lift out the hijiki with your hands, squeeze out the excess water, and chop coarsely.

2. Melt the butter in a skillet over medium-high heat. Add the snow peas and stir constantly for 2 minutes. Add the garlic and the hijiki, stirring until the snow peas are bright green and the garlic is fragrant. Add the salt, stir, and serve.

Arame lightly seasons the sweet vegetable mixture, while providing a compatibly tender texture for the cabbage. The walnuts and currants add a contrast of flavors and crunch inside these inviting rolled leaves. This dish can also be served as a finger food if each stuffed cabbage is sliced into three pieces.

If the head of Napa cabbage is small, double the number of leaves. The leaves should be about 5 inches wide.

Serve with grilled chicken.

Stuffed Chinese Cabbage

Makes 4 servings

1¼ cups arame

9 large Napa cabbage leaves

2 tablespoons toasted sesame oil

1 large onion, cut into 1-inch pieces

2 carrots, cut into 2-inch matchsticks

2 ribs celery, minced

½ cup currants

2 tablespoons tamari

1 tablespoon mirin

1½ cup walnuts, toasted (see page 64) and coarsely chopped

1. Rinse the arame in a bowl with cool water for 10 seconds. Drain and set aside.

2. Bring 6 cups of water to a boil. Starting from the bottom of each cabbage leaf, cut a 2-inch inverted V, removing the thick, tough midsection. Add 3 of the cabbage leaves to the boiling water and boil for 3 to 4 minutes until the leaves are wilted and pliable. Drain well and set aside. Repeat until all the leaves are cooked. Reserve the cooking water.

3. Heat the oil in a large skillet over medium heat for 15 seconds. Add the onion and cook 2 minutes, until transparent. Add the arame, carrots, celery, and currants, stirring to mix the vegetables and arame well. Add 2½ cups of the reserved cooking water, the tamari, and mirin. Bring to a boil, lower the heat, and simmer for 30 minutes, or until the liquid has evaporated and the vegetables are tender. Transfer to a large bowl to cool, about 15 minutes. Add the walnuts.

4. Place a cabbage leaf on a cutting board with the point of the inverted V closest to you. Spoon 3 heaping tablespoons of the arame/vegetable mixture into the middle of the leaf. Lift the end closest to you and fold it over the mound. Fold the outer edges in toward the center, and continue rolling away from you until you reach the end of the leaf. Set aside and repeat until all the leaves are filled. Serve on a platter or cut the rolls into 2 or 3 pieces and serve cut side up.

Look for Eden brand Sesame Seaweed Sprinkle in the health food store. It is a combination of brown and black sesame seeds, nori flakes, and shiso leaves. Use it on vegetables, grains, tofu, chicken, or fish. For a nuttier flavor in this recipe, substitute 2 teaspoons walnut oil for the butter.

Simply String Beans

Makes 4 servings

1 pound string beans, trimmed

Pinch of sea salt

1 tablespoon butter

2 tablespoons Eden Sesame Seaweed Sprinkle

1. Bring 2 cups water and the salt to a boil.

2. Add the string beans and blanch for 4 minutes until the beans are bright green and still have some crunch. (Since string beans grow in various sizes, boiling times differ.) Drain. Put the string beans in a serving bowl, add the butter, and toss. Sprinkle on the sesame-seaweed mix and toss.

Beans that have been cooked and refrigerated overnight make the best refried beans. Choose your favorite beans—pinto, black, kidney, navy. Bullwhip kelp softens quickly, adds a mellow briny flavor, and its own bright green color. Serve with rice and greens.

Frijoles Refritos (Refried Beans)

Makes 4 servings

2 tablespoons extra virgin olive oil

1 onion, coarsely chopped

2 jalapeños, seeded and minced

4 cloves garlic, minced

2 teaspoons ground cumin

½ cup medium chunky salsa or
1 large tomato, coarsely chopped

4 cups cooked beans, or
two 15-ounce cans beans,
drained and rinsed well

½ cup bullwhip kelp, lightly crushed
(not rinsed)

1. Heat the oil in a large skillet over medium heat. Add the onion, jalapeños, and garlic. Sauté until the onion is transparent, 2 to 3 minutes. Add the cumin and stir until the mixture is fragrant and the vegetables are coated with the spice, about 45 seconds. Pour in the salsa (or add the tomato) and stir. Add the beans as a solid layer and do not stir. Sprinkle the kelp over the beans and let cook for 5 minutes before stirring.

2. Pour a small amount of water over the beans as needed to prevent them from burning. Cook another 10 minutes over low heat or until the beans are heated thoroughly.

Ito wakame, which is lighter green and more tender than wakame, requires very little or no cooking and brings a delicate, sweet-salty flavor to mild asparagus. Though ito becomes tender, it holds its shape. This side dish can become a vegetarian entree served over a light grain, such as couscous or bulgur. It's my personal favorite in the spring when asparagus are fresh and tender. It gets its scrumptious flavor from the combination of the ito with shallots, garlic, and lemon.

If ito wakame is not available, wakame can be substituted, but it will be darker and more chewy than ito. If you are using wakame, add it soaked but not sautéed in step 3.

Asparagus with Wakame

Makes 4 servings

½ cup dried ito wakame

1½ pounds asparagus, trimmed, cut into 1-inch pieces

2 tablespoons extra virgin olive oil

3 shallots, minced

4 cloves garlic, minced

½ teaspoon sea salt

Juice of ½ lemon

Dash of black pepper

Sprinkle of grated Parmesan

1. Rinse the ito wakame under cool running water for 5 seconds. Soak in fresh cool water to cover for 15 minutes. Lift it out with your hands and chop it into coarse pieces.

2. In a large pot, bring 2 inches of water to a boil and add the asparagus. Cook until bright green and tender, about 3 minutes. Drain and set aside.

3. Heat the oil and sauté the chopped ito wakame for 2 minutes, stirring several times. Add the shallots, garlic, and salt. Sauté for 3 minutes. Add the asparagus, lemon juice, and pepper and sauté until the lemon juice is evaporated, 5 to 7 minutes.

Serve topped with freshly grated Parmesan.

Dried dulse is eaten as a snack in Ireland. This variation of a traditional Irish potato dish incorporates garlic-dulse flakes, a ready-made condiment, available at most health food stores. Dulse's salty, spicy strength gives potatoes a boost of seasoning and a speckled burgundy appearance. The flavor of dulse intensifies the longer it remains in a dish. If you prepare this dish in advance, its presence will be more distinct.

Serve with any of your favorite entrees when you crave a potato side.

Dulse Mashed Potatoes

Makes 4 servings

2 pounds new potatoes with skin, cut in half

7 large cloves garlic, whole

½ teaspoon sea salt

4 tablespoons butter

1 cup heavy cream

1 teaspoon garlic-dulse flakes

Black pepper to taste

1. Put the potatoes, garlic, and salt in a pot and cover with cold water. Bring to a boil. Lower the heat and simmer for 30 minutes, until the potatoes are tender in the center.

2. Drain any remaining liquid. Add the butter while mashing the potatoes with a fork, potato masher, or ricer.

3. Gently stir in the cream and garlic-dulse flakes. Season with salt and pepper to taste.

Variations

New potatoes are more tender and sweet than other potatoes. Their skins are thin, and leaving them on adds texture. If you prefer, you can simply peel them after cooking. You may also substitute other potatoes, but they should be peeled.

For a more robust garlic flavor, trim the top off a bulb of garlic to expose the cloves. Drizzle a teaspoon of olive oil on top, put the bulb in a baking dish, and roast it in a preheated oven at 375°F for 30 minutes. The cloves will be soft and tender, like a ripe avocado. Add them to the potatoes while mashing.

If you prefer to lower the fat, substitute the milk of your choice or unflavored soy milk for the heavy cream.

This Southern favorite, with its sweet, tender beans and corn, welcomes the mild saltiness of wakame. No milk is needed, as the wakame becomes creamy and adds body. Make the dish as spicy as you like by adding hot sauce.

Fava beans or frozen limas may be substituted if fresh lima beans are not available.

Wakame Succotash

Makes 4 servings

⅓ cup wakame

2 tablespoons corn oil

1 large onion, minced

2 cups cooked lima beans

2 cups corn kernels

1 red bell pepper, chopped

2 teaspoons dried basil

2 teaspoons dried oregano

1 teaspoon dried thyme

2 teaspoons sea salt

Hot sauce to taste

1. Rinse the wakame under cool water for 5 seconds, then cover with cool water to soak for 15 minutes. Lift it out with your hands and finely chop. Set aside.

2. Heat the oil in a large skillet over medium heat for 10 seconds and sauté the onion until golden brown, about 5 minutes.

3. Stir in the limas, corn, and bell pepper, mixing them well with the onions. Add the wakame, herbs, and salt and stir for 2 minutes until the herbs have coated the vegetables.

4. Pour 1½ cups water into the skillet and bring to a boil. Lower the heat and simmer for 5 minutes. The wakame should be creamy. Transfer to a serving bowl. Pass the hot sauce.

This half-dollar-size, sweet, savory, and crunchy finger food mingles well with many an entree. My husband says the flavor reminds him of latkes.

Fucus Tip Crisps

Makes 16 half-dollar-size crisps

1 cup rolled oats

¾ cup fucus tips

¼ cup finely grated raw buttercup squash with peel on

2 tablespoons minced onion

½ teaspoon sea salt

¼ teaspoon mild hot sauce

¼ teaspoon garlic-dulse flakes

¼ cup extra virgin olive oil

1 tablespoon butter

1. In a medium bowl, pour ½ cup cold water over the rolled oats and let them sit for 30 minutes.

2. Rinse the fucus tips in a small bowl of water. Lift them out with your hands and discard the water. Put the fucus back in the bowl with 1 cup fresh cool water. Soak for 15 minutes. Lift the seaweed out of the water and chop coarsely.

3. Add the fucus tips, squash, onion, salt, hot sauce, and garlic-dulse flakes to the bowl of soaked oats. Stir well. The mixture will become sticky from the fucus and wet oats. Chill for 15 minutes.

4. Heat a skillet with the oil and butter over medium heat for 3 minutes. Using a tablespoon, scoop out the oat and fucus mixture and drop gently into the hot oil. Fry on each side until golden brown, 3 to 4 minutes. Drain on paper towels. Serve warm.

Rolls, Wraps, and Sandwiches

When lightly toasted, dulse is less salty. In a low-temperature oven, it becomes crisp and similar in texture to thinly sliced fried bacon. Toasted dulse can also be added to wraps.

This delicious, mineral-packed version of the traditional BLT is a fast sandwich, adaptable to any of your favorite fillings. Stack them high or low, depending on your sense of adventure! Individual ingredients can be prepared ahead of time. The dressing becomes more flavorful the longer it sits. Don't forget the chips and drinks!

DLTs (Dulse, Lettuce, and Tomato Sandwiches)

Makes 5 sandwiches

2 cups loosely packed dried dulse
1 head green leaf lettuce
1 package alfalfa or sunflower sprouts
2 tomatoes, thinly sliced
Sourdough French bread, thinly sliced

For the horseradish spread

1 cup mayonnaise or tofu mayonnaise
¼ red onion, minced
1 tablespoon grated horseradish,
or to taste

1. Preheat the oven to 300°F. Open up the pieces of dulse and remove any tiny seashells.

2. Spread the dulse on a baking sheet in a single layer. Bake for 4 to 7 minutes, until lightly browned. Put in a bowl until ready to use.

3. Blend all the horseradish spread ingredients well. Refrigerate at least 30 minutes.

4. Spread the horseradish mayonnaise on bread. Build sandwiches with lettuce, sprouts, tomato, and dulse.

Nori is the classic sea vegetable used in norimaki preparations. Sheet nori, when dry, is quite crispy. It becomes tender and slightly elastic when moistened and is, therefore, well suited for rolling pasta, grains, and vegetables. Nori's green color contrasts beautifully with rolled-up ingredients, allowing for great variety in presentation.

Any long pasta works well for this recipe. Udon, a Japanese rice flour and wheat noodle, is thick and easy to roll. There are many flavorful new pastas on the market. Experiment and find your favorites.

Umeboshi paste is pickled, pureed Japanese plums. Its flavor is concentrated, both salty and sour. It complements the mustard flavor. A small amount goes a long way.

Noodle rolls are excellent for many occasions. Include any of your favorite foods. One of the tricks to making a tight roll with noodles is simply to drain the noodles well after boiling.

You will need a sushi mat to make the rolls.

Nori Pasta Rolls

Makes 6 rolls to be cut into 5 pieces each

4 to 6 sheets toasted nori

8-ounce package udon noodles, boiled and drained (do not rinse!)

1 tablespoon umeboshi paste

1 to 2 tablespoons stone-ground mustard, to taste

1 red bell pepper, cut into long thin strips

2 avocados, thinly sliced

2 carrots, peeled, cut into long thin strips, boiled for 30 seconds, and drained

½ lemon

1. Put the nori with the creases parallel to the threads of the sushi mat. Take a handful of cooked noodles and place on the nori at the end closest to you. Using a knife, spread about ½ teaspoon umeboshi paste and up to 1 teaspoon mustard across the top of the noodles in a 1-inch band across the width.

2. Place several strips of bell pepper, avocado, and carrot on top of the paste. Lift the edge of the nori near you and tuck the nori edge under the noodles.

3. Roll the nori away from you, pulling tightly to secure the mound of noodles in the roll. Place the rolled nori, seam side down, on a cutting board several minutes prior to cutting to complete the roll.

4. Cut it into pieces of the desired size with a sharp, wet knife. The moisture keeps the knife from getting sticky from the filling as each cut is made. For an attractive presentation, the nori rolls can be cut on an angle.

Note: These can be made a day ahead of time. The key to maintaining freshness is keeping them whole and wrapped tightly in plastic until the rolls are ready to be eaten. Cut them when ready to serve. To retain the beautiful green color of the avocados after cutting, squeeze a small amount of lemon juice on them. It retards browning.

Ito wakame will retain its vibrant green during light cooking, yet softens to resemble the texture of eggs. The eggs have a slight salty flavor and sparkle with sea color when cooked with wakame. The hot sauce and watercress heat up the combination.

Brunch Burrito

Makes 4 servings

½ cup lightly packed ito wakame

8 eggs

¼ cup milk

1 teaspoon mild hot sauce

Pinch of sea salt

4 whole wheat burritos

1 tablespoon extra virgin olive oil

Mayonnaise, ketchup, or other condiments

1 bunch watercress, rinsed, dried, and stemmed

1. Preheat the oven to 325°F.

2. Rinse the ito wakame under cool running water for 5 seconds. Place in a bowl with cool water to cover and soak for 20 minutes. Drain. Rinse again. Lift it out with your hands and squeeze. Chop coarsely. Set aside.

3. Whisk together the eggs, milk, hot sauce, and salt. Stir in the chopped wakame.

4. Place the burritos in the oven for 5 minutes, or until thoroughly warmed but still moist.

5. Heat the oil in a nonstick skillet for 5 seconds. Pour in the egg mixture. After a minute, move the eggs around, using a plastic spatula. Repeat until the eggs are cooked through. They should look solid, with no wet places.

Add condiments of choice to the burritos and fill the centers with a generous amount of watercress.

Add eggs, fold, and serve immediately.

This mild sea vegetable—arame—cooked with corn and baked in crispy dough is a contrast of flavors and textures. The arame cooked in this sweet gingery sauce is a contrast to the crispy phyllo wrapping.

The best way to eat these is with your hands. A salad with a vinaigrette dressing placed in the center of a serving plate goes well the rolls.

Baked Sea Vegetable Rolls

Makes 2 phyllo rolls (16 pieces each)

5 cups loosely packed arame

4 tablespoons butter melted, plus some for brushing phyllo

2 red onions, cut into 1-inch pieces

⅓ cup tamari

¼ cup pure maple syrup

¼ cup apple juice

3 tablespoons ginger juice

3 cups corn kernels, fresh or frozen

Half a 1-pound package phyllo dough

1. Preheat the oven to 350°F.

2. Rinse the arame in a bowl with cool water for 5 seconds. Drain. Cover with cool water and soak for 10 minutes. Lift out with your hands and squeeze out excess water. Set aside.

3. In a large skillet, melt the 4 tablespoons butter and sauté the onions until golden, about 5 minutes. Put the arame on top of the onions. Pour 4 cups water, the tamari, maple syrup, and apple juice into the skillet. Bring to a boil, lower the heat, and simmer with the lid off until most of the liquid has evaporated, about 30 minutes. The onions and arame will have a sheen and the remaining liquid will be slightly thick. Add the ginger juice and corn kernels. Simmer for 3 minutes and remove from the heat. Let cool completely to prevent the phyllo from getting soggy in the next step.

4. Prepare the phyllo dough by buttering 6 individual sheets of the dough with a pastry brush. Stack the sheets of dough on top of one another as you oil them.

5. Put half of the arame mixture into a 3-inch-high mound that extends across the width of the dough, leaving 2 inches open on each end. Lift the edge closest to you and wrap it around the band of the arame mixture, working quickly, tucking its edge under the mixture. Continue rolling the dough away from you until the top edge is tightly rolled. Leave the corners open. Repeat steps 4 and 5 for the other half of the arame mixture.

6. Place the phyllo rolls on a baking sheet. Bake until light golden, 15 to 25 minutes. Transfer to a wire rack and let cool completely before slicing. Using a sharp knife, cut quickly through the phyllo dough, making 2-inch-wide pieces. The end pieces will be extra crunchy. To serve, place the interior side of the sliced rolls up so the sweet arame and vegetable mixture is visible.

Dulse softens in the oil and adds body to the basil and garlic. The spicy and smoky flavor makes you want more and more. When I make this, most of it gets eaten by bread dippers before I get to use it for anything else!

Great here with fresh tomatoes and hearty bread, it also adds great flavor to chicken, turkey, tofu, or vegetable pita sandwiches. It can also be brushed on grilled vegetables just prior to serving.

Smoked Dulse and Basil Infusion

Makes 2 cups

¼ cup tightly packed smoked dulse

1½ cups extra virgin olive oil

½ bulb garlic, cloves peeled and minced

12 medium basil leaves, coarsely chopped

2 tomatoes, thinly sliced

Italian or French bread, cut in ½-inch slices

1. Rinse the dulse under cool running water for a few seconds, then squeeze out excess water. Chop into coarse pieces.

2. In a glass jar, combine the oil, garlic, basil, and dulse. Close the jar and let sit at room temperature for 1 to 2 hours before using. To serve, assemble tomato slices atop the bread on a platter with the infusion in a bowl in the center with a spoon. Refrigerated, this will keep for 10 days.

Note: Roasted garlic can be substituted for the garlic.

Rosemary with Alaria Infusion

¼ cup tightly packed alaria

¼ teaspoon sea salt

2 sprigs rosemary, leaves removed and coarsely chopped to make about 2 tablespoons

1. Rinse the alaria well in cool water for 15 seconds, then cover with cool water and soak for 10 minutes. Lift it out with your hands, squeeze out excess water, and chop into coarse pieces.

2. In a glass jar, combine the oil, garlic, salt, alaria, and rosemary.

The salty essence of nori flakes complements the sweet filling in these crepes.

Maple sugar crystals are dehydrated maple syrup. They can be used like granulated sugar, but the flavor is milder. Chickpea miso is a paste made from fermented chickpeas. Its flavor is sweet, mild, and salty. Both can be purchased from specialty shops and most health food stores.

Crispy Crepes with Nori Flakes

Makes 8 crepes

2 teaspoons nori flakes

¾ cup all-purpose flour

2 egg whites

1 cup milk or soy milk

1 tablespoon coconut oil plus enough to thinly coat the skillet

2 teaspoons maple sugar crystals

½ teaspoon pure vanilla extract

For the filling

2 teaspoons coconut oil

4 Granny Smith apples, peeled and cut into ½-inch cubes

½ cup currants

1 teaspoon chickpea miso, mixed with 2 teaspoons water until creamy

¼ cup pure maple syrup

¼ teaspoon grated orange zest

2 teaspoons arrowroot, diluted in 2 tablespoons water

1. Put the nori flakes and flour in a medium mixing bowl. Whisk in the egg white and ½ cup of the milk; continue whisking until smooth. Whisk in the oil, maple crystals, vanilla, and the remaining ½ cup milk. The batter should be thin.

2. Pour a thin coat of oil in an 8-inch nonstick skillet and heat on high for 5 to 10 seconds. Pour 3 tablespoons batter in the skillet and quickly tilt and shake the skillet until the entire surface is covered with a thin layer. Cook the crepe over medium heat for 30 to 40 seconds until it is brown on the bottom. Using a fork, lift the crepe along one side, quickly grab it with both hands, and gently flip it over in the skillet. Finish cooking for 20 to 30 seconds. Repeat this process until all are cooked. Stack the crepes covered with a cloth to keep them warm or place them in a 225°F oven.

3. In the same skillet, heat the coconut oil over medium heat. Add the apples and stir until they are slightly softened, about 5 minutes. Add the currants, miso, syrup, and zest. Lower the heat and simmer for 5 minutes, until the apples are soft but still have their shape. Add the arrowroot and continue to stir until thickened and shiny, 3 to 5 minutes. Place a tablespoon of the apple mixture in the center of each crepe and fold the crepe over it. Serve warm.

Sandwich ideas for sea vegetables

Avocado and hijiki • Dulse and tuna • Nori sheets and fried eggs • Bullwhip kelp, cucumbers, and watercress • Arame and tofu • Dulse and arugula • Any sea vegetable and tempeh

Breads that go well with sea vegetable sandwiches

French • Italian • Sourdough • Pitas

Ingredients that go well with sea vegetable sandwiches

Stone-ground mustard • Tofu or traditional mayonnaise • Tahini • Hot sauce • Horseradish spread

Condiments

For these pickles, kelp packaged as "wild Atlantic kombu" can be used. The kelp will maintain its natural firm texture and crunch while being pickled. The umeboshi vinegar serves as a pickling agent. Umeboshi vinegar is not a true vinegar but the brine of Japanese pickled plums. It has a salty and sour flavor and is much more concentrated than other vinegars. It is available in Asian markets and health food stores.

These spicy, salty pickles are delicious over eggs, as a topping for quick salads, sandwich fillers, or simply in a bowl on the table to which everyone can help themselves.

They will last two weeks refrigerated in a glass jar, though they become stronger and more concentrated with time. If the flavor is too intense, rinse with cold water in a bowl, then drain before eating.

Pickled Kelp

Makes 1½ cups or 8 servings

1 ounce dried kelp

½ cup tamari

2 tablespoons umeboshi vinegar

1 tablespoon pure maple syrup

1 shallot, minced

3 cloves garlic, minced

1. Rinse the kelp in cool water for 5 seconds, then cover with cool water and soak for 10 minutes. Avoid oversoaking the kelp, as it gets slippery and difficult to slice. Lift it out with your hands and slice into ½-inch-wide strips. Set aside.

2. Pour the tamari, vinegar, and maple syrup into a glass jar. Stir well with a fork and add the shallot and garlic. Stir again. Add the kelp and mix. Let the mixture sit at room temperature for an hour, then cover and refrigerate. The pickles will be ready in 24 hours.

Pickled Kelp, Spicy Sea Vegetable Kimchee, Dulse Relish

Sheet nori prepared this way is creamy, rich, and reminiscent of creamed spinach in appearance and texture, only darker. This nutrient-dense condiment goes well atop warm grains. It is also delicious served on its own. It will stay fresh several days refrigerated. Bring to room temperature prior to serving.

For ginger juice, you'll need a flat, handheld, stainless steel grater, or a ceramic ginger grater.

Nori Condiment

Makes 2 cups or eight ¼-cup servings

10 sheets toasted nori,
torn into small pieces

3½ tablespoons shoyu

2½ tablespoons pure maple syrup

1 small onion, minced

2-inch piece fresh ginger

¾ teaspoon toasted sesame oil

1. Place the nori in a small pot with 1¾ cups water. Let sit for 10 minutes.

2. Grate the ginger into a half-dollar-size mound. Using cheesecloth or your hand, squeeze the juice into a small bowl. Discard the pulp. Add the shoyu, maple syrup, and onion to the nori. Bring the pot to a boil over medium heat. Boil for 10 minutes, stirring frequently. Lower the heat and add the ginger juice and oil. Simmer for 10 minutes. Serve warm or at room temperature.

Variation

If you cannot find toasted nori, use it untoasted. Or you can toast nori over the low flame of a stovetop burner. Quickly and carefully glide a single sheet of nori across the flame, alternating sides. If you have an electric stovetop, a flame-tamer will prevent the nori from burning easily. Place a heat diffuser on the burner of your stove and set the heat on the lowest setting. Glide the nori sheet back and forth across the heat diffuser. Work quickly to avoid burning the nori.

I love the sweetness of the yellow pepper with the iron-rich salty flavor of dulse in this relish. It's a mouthwatering topping for burgers, wrapped foods, simple grains, and pastas. Make extra, as it's a real crowd pleaser.

Dulse Relish

Makes 4 servings

½ **cup tightly packed dulse**

1 **yellow bell pepper, seeded and cut in small dice**

1 **teaspoon mirin**

2 **tablespoons pure maple syrup**

¼ **cup coarsely chopped cilantro**

¼ **teaspoon sea salt**

1. Rinse the dulse under cool water for 10 seconds. Squeeze it dry and chop coarsely.

2. Put the bell pepper and dulse in a bowl and drizzle the mirin and maple syrup over them. Mix well. Add the cilantro and salt and toss. Let sit at room temperature for 20 minutes prior to serving.

Note: This can be prepared in advance and refrigerated overnight. It will stay fresh for 3 to 4 days, covered and refrigerated.

Variation for the summer

Grill 3 ears of corn and remove the kernels to replace the bell pepper. When using corn, you may also mix in 3 tablespoons of extra virgin olive oil.

This, like all the seaweed sprinkles, is highly nutritious food with concentrated flavor. It is simple to prepare. I make small batches and leave it on the table in a jar, so my family can help themselves to a sprinkle over grains, pasta, fish, and chicken.

The sprinkle will remain fresh unrefrigerated for one to two weeks.

To make this you will need a suribachi (japanese mortar and pestle with a textured surface for easier grinding) or a spice grinder.

Pumpkin Seed Dulse Sprinkle

Makes 1¾ cups

1½ cups pumpkin seeds
¼ cup loosely packed dulse

1. Put the pumpkin seeds in a strainer and quickly rinse under cool running water for 10 seconds. Drain well.

2. Heat a small skillet for 20 seconds over medium heat and put in the seeds. Using a wooden spoon, stir the seeds constantly, 5 to 8 minutes, until they puff up and make a low popping sound.

3. Transfer the hot seeds to a suribachi or spice grinder and grind until powdery. Pour into a bowl.

4. Tear the dulse into small pieces and place in the skillet used to toast the seeds. Over very low heat, stir the dulse until it turns light brown, 3 to 5 minutes. Transfer the dulse to the suribachi or spice grinder and process until powdery. Add to the pumpkin seeds and mix well. When cool, pour into a jar.

Kimchee is Korean preserved vegetables. It is served at every meal, and a Korean meal without kimchee is not a meal at all! It can be eaten with a meal or chopped small and put into omelets, sandwiches, pastas, and grains.

Traditionally, kimchee contains an assortment of vegetables, often seasonal and almost always including garlic, ginger, red hot chiles, salt, dried and fresh fish, and spices. Occasionally, seaweed is used.

In this kimchee, I have included several sea vegetables for their flavors and nutritional values. It lasts up to a week, refrigerated.

Spicy Sea Vegetable Kimchee

Makes 1 quart

¼ cup kiri kombu

¼ cup sea palm

1½ tablespoons rice flour

6 radishes, thinly sliced

1 Napa cabbage, cut into 2-inch pieces

1½ cups watercress, rinsed, dried, and cut into 1-inch pieces

10 scallions, cut into 2-inch pieces

⅓ cup minced garlic

¼ cup ginger, peeled and minced

½ cup red hot chili powder

½ cup sea salt

1. Rinse the kiri kombu with cool water for 10 seconds, then cover with water and soak for 10 minutes. Lift it out with your hands and cut into 2-inch pieces. Use the same procedure for the sea palm.

2. Dissolve the rice flour in 1¼ cups water. Bring to a boil and let cool. It will look milky. Set aside.

3. In a large glass bowl, mix the radishes, cabbage, watercress, scallions, kombu, and sea palm. Set aside.

4. Blend the garlic, ginger, and chili powder in a food processor for 1 minute. Add 2 cups water to the blender and blend for 30 seconds. Then whisk this mixture into 2 cups water, adding the rice flour–water mixture and salt. Pour this mixture over the vegetables and mix well. Transfer to a quart glass jar with lid. Refrigerate for 24 hours.

This is a tasty, nutritious condiment for grains, fresh salads, pastas, and lightly cooked vegetables. Its nutty flavor and fragrance quickly liven up any dish. It can be left on the table where everyone can help themselves to a sprinkle of the seeds. A serving is 1 to 2 teaspoons. The sprinkle will stay fresh for 10 days in a glass jar unrefrigerated.

Sesame Wakame Sprinkle

Makes 1 cup

8-inch piece dried wakame or alaria

1 cup brown sesame seeds

1. Cut the wakame into tiny pieces with scissors. (You will have about 2 tablespoons.)

2. Heat a skillet over low heat. Add the wakame and stir occasionally for 10 minutes until it darkens and produces a salty fragrance.

3. Put the wakame in a spice grinder and grind to a fine powder. Pour into a bowl.

4. Lightly rinse the sesame seeds in a fine-mesh strainer with cool running water for 15 seconds and drain well. Tapping the bottom of the strainer several times helps remove excess water.

5. In the same warm skillet used for the wakame, toast the sesame seeds over low heat for 8 to 10 minutes, stirring frequently with a wooden spoon, until dry and light golden brown. Transfer to a small bowl to cool.

6. In small batches, grind the seeds in a spice grinder until powdery. Add to the bowl with the wakame powder. Stir. When it's completely cool, store the mixture in a jar.

I keep a coffee grinder just for grinding spices, herbs, seeds, and nuts. This way the coffee does not impart any flavors. A mortar and pestle or Japanese suribachi (a bowl with a textured surface) may be used instead of a coffee grinder to grind the wakame and seeds. It is quicker, though, with a small coffee grinder.

This pungent sea vegetable is rounded out by pumpkin seed oil's richness and the sweetness of maple syrup. Eat small amounts alongside salty foods.

Sweetened Sea Lettuce Condiment

Makes 1 cup or 4 servings

1 cup sea lettuce

2 tablespoons pumpkin seed oil

½ teaspoon umeboshi vinegar

1 teaspoon pure maple syrup

1. Rinse the sea lettuce in a bowl of warm water for 5 seconds. Drain and repeat. Cover with 2 cups of warm water and soak for 30 minutes. Lift the sea vegetable out of the water with your hands and squeeze all the water out.

2. Finely chop the sea lettuce and place in a small bowl. Add the oil, vinegar, and syrup. Stir well. Refrigerate for 2 to 3 days.

Sweets
and Treats

Super for munching, the nori flakes balance the flavor of the sweet ingredients. These are reminiscent of sweet, crunchy candy bars from childhood. They are sticky, chewy, and fun to make with kids.

This treat is sweetened with barley malt, a sweetener prepared from barley grain. Its color and texture resemble molasses, but it is much less sweet. It can be purchased in health food stores.

Crispy Rice Treats

Makes 6 servings

3 cups puffed rice cereal

1 cup unsalted roasted peanuts

¼ cup raw sunflower seeds

1 cup raisins

1 tablespoon nori flakes

1 cup barley malt

½ cup pure maple syrup

1 teaspoon pure vanilla extract

2 teaspoons tahini

½ cup unsalted peanut butter

2 teaspoons coconut oil or canola oil

1. Preheat the oven to 325°F.

2. In a large mixing bowl combine the puffed cereal, peanuts, sunflower seeds, raisins and nori flakes. Mix and set aside.

3. Heat a medium saucepan on low heat and add 1 cup of water. Add the barley malt, maple syrup, vanilla, tahini, and peanut butter. Using a whisk, stir constantly until the consistency is uniform, 5 to 8 minutes, being careful not to boil or burn the mixture.

4. Pour the hot mixture across the cereal mixture. Using a wooden spoon, coat the dry ingredients well with the liquid mixture. It will be sticky! Wet your hands with cool water and mix again, using your hands. Mixing will become progressively easier, and the mixture more uniform.

5. Oil a 12-inch baking pan with the coconut oil. The pan should be very oily to make it easier to remove the mixture after baking. With wet hands, press the mixture into the dish. Bake for 20 to 30 minutes, until brown. Remove from the oven and let cool. As the mixture cools it will harden. Remove with a spatula. Serve cut in squares or break it like peanut brittle.

A rich hazelnut cream confection, with a hint of orange essence, this dessert can be dressed up or served alone. To dress it up, pour the mousse into tall parfait glasses and top with whipped cream. Garnish the cream with nuts. For quick serving, pour the mousse into small colorful bowls and garnish.

Hazelnut Mousse

Makes 4 servings

5 tablespoons agar flakes

3 cups apple juice

½ cup pure maple syrup

¼ teaspoon pure orange extract

2 tablespoons instant decaffeinated coffee flakes, or roasted grain coffee, such as *Paro* or *Coffix*

3 tablespoons hazelnut butter

2 cups toasted, chopped hazelnuts, for garnish

1. Soak the agar flakes in ½ cup of warm water for 10 minutes.

2. In a saucepan, slowly bring the apple juice, 1 cup water, the maple syrup, and the soaked agar flakes to a boil. Reduce the heat, and simmer until the agar is dissolved, about 20 minutes, or until there are no longer any visible agar flakes. Stir in the orange extract and instant coffee.

3. Pour the hot liquid into a shallow pan to cool. When steam is no longer present, place the pan in the refrigerator to gel, about an hour.

4. Put half of the gelled mixture into a blender. Add half of the hazelnut butter and blend well.

5. Repeat the process with the remaining mixture. Pour into serving bowls and garnish with chopped nuts.

Agar is a tasteless, odorless natural gelatin that comes from the sea. It has virtually no calories. It is great when you need to "set" desserts such as mousse or aspic, often referred to as kanten. When cow's milk, nut milks, or grain milks are used with agar, as in this recipe, it is best to soak the agar in water first, then add it to the milk. (Milk can cause agar to toughen slightly before it dissolves while heating or if heated quickly.)

Kanten means "cold sky." The name refers to natural overnight drying methods. Its texture is firm, yet tender. It's a quick, light, refreshing dessert, especially great for summer because it requires little cooking—keeping your kitchen cool. Summer is also the time for scrumptious berries. You can vary the fruit according to availability. Melons cut into cubes are equally delicious.

After kanten has "set," a portion of it can be lightly blended and added like cream to the top. Another way to serve this dessert is to blend all of the "set" kanten and serve it as a mousse, topped with fresh berries.

Present this dessert in individual bowls or let people help themselves from one large, brightly colored bowl for a bolder effect.

Three-Berry Kanten

Makes 5 servings

⅓ **cup agar flakes**
4 **cups apricot juice**
1 **teaspoon pure vanilla extract**
¼ **cup pure maple syrup**
¼ **cup heavy cream**
1 **cup fresh raspberries**
1 **cup fresh blueberries**
6 **strawberries, thinly sliced**

1. Place the agar in a bowl and add enough warm water just to cover the flakes. Let it sit for 10 to 15 minutes. Agar does not dissolve like instant coffee. Rather, it absorbs liquid first and swells. It will look like transparent beads. After swelling, the agar will dissolve when heated.

2. Place the juice and the dissolved agar in a pot. Let sit for 10 minutes.

3. Gently heat the juice and agar, whisking several times, as you bring the mixture to a boil. Lower the heat and simmer for 10 minutes. Add the vanilla, maple syrup, and heavy cream and stir to combine. Remove from the heat.

4. Divide the berries into portions and place in glass serving bowls. Using a ladle, fill the bowls or goblets three-quarters full with the hot juice. Let the bowls sit until there is no longer any steam rising. Place in the refrigerator until the kanten is firm, 30 to 40 minutes. (Agar flakes will not thicken or set until chilled, so you do not have to hurry when filling the bowls.)

This is one of my family's favorite nibbles for traveling. Bullwhip kelp adds crunch and a salty-sweetness to the toasted nuts, seeds, and dried fruits. Better tasting than a bag of chips.

Trail Mix

Makes 4 cups

**2 cups bullwhip kelp,
lightly crushed (not rinsed)**

**1½ cups toasted almonds,
coarsely chopped
(see Note, page 64)**

½ cup toasted sunflower seeds

½ cup chopped dried apples

½ cup currants

In a mixing bowl or zippered plastic bag, combine all the ingredients well.

Note: If the bullwhip kelp has become moist, place it on a baking sheet first and heat in a 250°F oven for 3 to 5 minutes to restore its crunch.

Variations

Substitute your favorite nuts, seeds, and dried fruit for the almonds, sunflower seeds, and currants. Nori can replace the bullwhip kelp. Tear 3 sheets of nori into small pieces and add to the other ingredients.

Just like gelatin, agar, a sea vegetable, sets the dessert. Agar has no flavor of its own to crowd out the sweet cider flavor and spices.

Apple Cider Gel

Makes 4 servings

4 tablespoons agar flakes

1 quart apple cider

5 cardamom pods

1 cinnamon stick

4 whole cloves

1 teaspoon grated lemon zest

¼ cup pure maple syrup

Whipped cream

4 sprigs mint or ½ cup fresh berries

1. In a pot, soak the agar flakes for 10 minutes in the apple cider. Bring the cider, agar, cardamom, cinnamon stick, and cloves to a boil, stirring with a whisk to help prevent the agar flakes from settling on the bottom of the pot. Reduce the heat to low and simmer for 15 minutes, to dissolve the agar. Remove the spices with tongs or a spoon and discard. Turn off the heat and stir in the lemon zest and maple syrup.

2. Pour the hot mixture into a small square pan, making a 1-inch layer of cider. Let the pan cool on the counter until there is no more steam rising, then refrigerate until firm to the touch, about 1½ hours. It will be firm like gelatin but opaque.

3. Cut the gel into 2-inch squares. Remove with a spatula, place in individual serving goblets, and top with several spoonfuls of whipped cream. Garnish with the mint or fresh berries.

Beauty Secrets from the Sea

Our great oceans have been harvested for seaweed, sea salt, and sea mud for centuries to cleanse, soften, and rejuvenate irritated, dry skin. The proteins, minerals, and vitamins in sea vegetables truly nourish and heal skin. Spas throughout the world offer seaweed wraps—enrobing the body in kelp and then warm blankets—so the skin can absorb nutrients while being softened and exfoliated.

Over-the-counter beauty products that contain seaweed extracts are widely available, including shampoos, conditioners, face soaps, lotions, masques, and bath gels.

Soaking in your bathtub with seaweed will make your skin feel clean, refreshed, and silky smooth. When you're tired, toss a handful of seaweed into your bath water and lie back luxuriantly. You'll emerge energized and sparkly clean. All bathing varieties of seaweed are available in bulk prices from Mendocino Sea Vegetable Company (see Mail-Order Sources).

After your bath, the seaweed can be dried and reused several times until it begins to break up and dissolve. To dry, hang the seaweed on hangers with clothespins. Place it in a netted bag until your next bath.

Mail-Order Sources

Acadian Sea Plants Limited

30 Brown Avenue, Dartmouth
Nova Scotia, Canada B3B1X8
902-468-2840
Fax 902-468-3474

*Edible sea vegetables and seaweed
ingredients for food, health, and beauty.
Call for catalogue.*

Carabay Seaweeds, Galway, Ireland

Kylebroughlan
Moycullen, Co. Galway
Ireland 00 35391 85112

*Harvests dulse, laver, and kelp and sells
wholesale and by mail.*

Eden Foods

701 Tecumseh Road
Clinton, MI 49236

*Produces snack foods using sea vegetables.
Their sea vegetable chips contain potato
starch, rice bran oil, wakame, kombu,
hijiki, and nori. Their norimaki rice
crackers are like mini pretzels, made from
sweet brown rice, nori, and tamari.*

Frontier

Box 299
Noway, IA 52318

*Packages bulk herbs and spices but
includes agar and Irish moss in weigh-
your-own displays.*

Maine Coast Sea Vegetable Company

3 Georges Pond Road
Franklin, ME 04634
207-565-2907
fax 207-565-2144
mcsv@seaveg.com
info@seaveg.com
www.seaveg.com

*Founded in 1971 by two people who
harvested 200 pounds of seaweed the first
year, this 15-person company now
produces more than 50,000 pounds
annually of alaria, dulse, kelp, and laver. It
also sells sea seasonings in shakers, sea
chips (tortilla chips seasoned with sea
vegetables), sea pickles, and snack bars.
Visit their excellent websites for more
information.*

Mendocino Sea Vegetable Company

P. O. Box 1265
Mendocino, CA 95460
707-895-2996

*A complete line of hand-harvested sea
vegetables—nori, wakame, kombu,
sea palm, dulse, fucus, grapestone,*

bladderwrack, sea lettuce, and kelp are supplied packaged and in bulk to individuals and retailers throughout the world. It has earned a well-deserved reputation for high-quality appearance, taste, and purity.

Rising Tide Sea Vegetables

P. O. Box 1914
Mendocino, CA 95460
707-964-5663
risingtide@mcn.org
www.loveseaweed.com

Hand-harvested beautiful, sweet kombu, sea palm, nori, and wakame dried in one continuous process, during which the seaweed is never allowed to rehydrate at all, which would cause the salts and sugars to come to the surface. The seaweed is packaged in airtight double or triple bags. These sea vegetables are noticeably more black and sweet than most other products because they are harvested in their prime

while still tender and unblemished. The company also imports several Japanese varieties. In addition, it produces snack items, including sea crunchies with almonds, maple kelp crunch bars, and ginger soynut kelp crunch bars.

Ryan Drum's Sweetwater Herb Farm

1525 Danby Mountain Road
Danby, VT 05739
and
Waldron Island, WA 98297

Hand-harvests bullwhip kelp and several other varieties of sea vegetables.

Sokensha Co. Ltd.

P. O. Box 883033
San Francisco, CA 94188

Importer of packaged sea vegetables from Japan. It produces a sea vegetable salad containing several varieties of wakame and agar to which you add water—it's ready to eat in 10 minutes.

Index

A

agar, about, 19–20, 119
age tofu in sea palm, 77
alaria:
    about, 20
    and rosemary infusion, 103
appetizers, 31–37
    arame-stuffed eggplants, 31
    California sea palm with polenta,
      35
    dulse-filled Irish soda muffins, 34
    hijiki crostini, 37
    kelp chips with horseradish dip, 32
apple cider gel, 122
arame:
    about, 21, 51
    -avocado guacamole, 51
    -stuffed eggplants, 31
    sweet, over baby artichokes, 67
artichokes, baby, sweet arame over,
    67
asparagus with wakame, 95
avocado-arame guacamole, 51

B

baked sea vegetable rolls, 102
barley malt, about, 116

basil and smoked dulse infusion, 103
basmati rice, 46
beans:
    refried, 93
    simply string, 92
bean soup:
    creamy white, 42
    Korean wakame and, 50
berry, three-, kanten, 119
black-eyed peas, wild nori in, 56
bonito and kombu stock (dashi), 49
brunch burrito, 101
Brussels sprouts with smoked dulse and
    water chestnuts, 84
bullwhip kelp, about, 22
burrito, brunch, 101

C

cabbage:
    with smoked dulse and water chestnuts,
      84
    stuffed Chinese, 90
Caesar salad, sea vegetable, 55
cannellini, in creamy white bean soup,
    42
carageenan (Irish moss), about, 25
cheese, goat, salad, smoked dulse and,
    53

chicken:
    kombumaki, 72
    noodle stew, 45
    sea palm salad, with roasted garlic, 63
    stroganoff, 73
chips, kelp, with horseradish dip, 32
cider, apple, gel, 122
citrus hijiki with roasted nuts, 64
coconut milk, creamy grapestone in, 85
condiments:
    dulse relish, 111
    nori, 110
    pickled kelp, 108
    pumpkin seed dulse sprinkle, 112
    sesame wakame sprinkle, 114
    spicy sea vegetable kimchee, 113
    sweetened sea lettuce, 115
crepes, crispy, with nori flakes, 104
crisps, fucus tip, 98
crostini, hijiki, 37
crunch 'n' brine salad, 60
curried sweet potato soup, 43

D

dashi (bonito and kombu stock), 49
dip, horseradish, kelp chips with, 32
DLTs (dulse, lettuce, and tomato sandwiches),
    99
dulse:
    about, 22–23
    -filled Irish soda muffins, 34
    lettuce and tomato sandwiches (DLTs), 99
    mashed potatoes, 96
    and pumpkin seed sprinkle, 112
    relish, 111

dulse, smoked:
    and basil infusion, 103
    and goat cheese salad, 53
    and water chestnuts, Brussels sprouts
        with, 84

E

eggplants, arame-stuffed, 31
entrées:
    age tofu in sea palm, 77
    chicken kombumaki, 72
    chicken stroganoff, 73
    fish en papillote, 79
    hijiki with deep-fried tempeh, 82
    mariscal with shrimp, 71
    nori-wrapped sole, 69
    roasted salmon steaks with kombu,
        74
    salmon cakes, 78
    sea vegetable tempura, 80
    sweet-and-sour tofu stir-fry, 70
    sweet arame over baby artichokes,
        67

F

fava bean soup, Italian, 48
fish:
    nori-wrapped sole, 69
    en papillote, 79
    roasted salmon steaks with kombu,
        74
    salmon cakes, 78
    Taiwanese fishermen's soup, 38

frijoles refritos (refried beans), 93
fucus tips:
    about, 23
    crisps, 98

G

garlic, roasted, sea palm chicken salad with,
    63
gel, apple cider, 122
goat cheese salad, smoked dulse and, 53
grapestone:
    about, 24
    creamy, in coconut milk, 85
guacamole, avocado-arame, 51

H

hazelnut mousse, 117
hijiki:
    about, 24–25
    citrus, with roasted nuts, 64
    crostini, 37
    with deep-fried tempeh, 82
    snow peas, 89
horseradish:
    dip, kelp chips with, 32
    spread, for DLTs, 99

I

infusions:
    rosemary with alaria, 103
    smoked dulse and basil, 103

Irish moss (carageenan), about, 25
Irish soda muffins, dulse-filled, 34
Italian fava bean soup, 48

J

jungle green salad with seeds, 66

K

kale, with seared shiitakes, 86
kanten, three-berry, 119
kelp:
    bullwhip, about, 22
    chips, with horseradish dip, 32
    pickled, 108
kimchee, spicy sea vegetable, 113
kombu:
    about, 26
    and bonito stock (dashi), 49
    roasted salmon steaks with, 74
kombumaki, chicken, 72
Korean wakame and beef soup,
    50

L

laver (wild nori), about, 27
lemongrass-shrimp-rice soup, 46
lemony spring vegetables, 83
lettuce:
    dulse and tomato sandwiches (DLTs),
    99
    sea, *see* sea lettuce

M

mariscal with shrimp, 71
milk, coconut, creamy grapestone in, 85
mirin, about, 21
miso soup, classic, 40
mousse, hazelnut, 117
muffins, dulse-filled Irish soda, 34

N

nori:
    about, 27–28
    condiment, 110
    flakes, crispy crepes with, 104
    pasta rolls, 100
    toasting of, 110
    wild, in black-eyed peas, 56
    -wrapped sole, 69
nuts, roasted, citrus hijiki with, 64

P

palm, *see* sea palm
papillote, fish en, 79
pasta:
    noodle, chicken, stew, 45
    rolls, nori, 100
peas:
    black-eyed, wild nori in, 56
    snow, hijiki, 89
pickled kelp, 108
polenta, California sea palm with, 35
potato, sweet, curried soup, 43

potatoes, dulse mashed, 96
pumpkin seed dulse sprinkle, 112

R

refried beans (frijoles refritos), 93
rice:
    basmati, 46
    brown, vinegar, about, 51
    -lemongrass-shrimp soup, 46
    treats, crispy, 116
rolls:
    baked sea vegetable, 102
    nori pasta, 100
rosemary with alaria infusion, 103

S

salad dressings:
    for sea palm chicken salad with roasted garlic, 63
    for sea vegetable Caesar salad, 55
    for spiced slaw, 54
salads:
    avocado-arame guacamole, 51
    citrus hijiki with roasted nuts, 64
    crunch 'n' brine, 60
    jungle green, with seeds, 66
    sea palm chicken, with roasted garlic, 63
    sea vegetable Caesar, 55
    smoked dulse and goat cheese, 53
    soba, 59
    spiced slaw, 54
    wild nori in black-eyed peas, 56

salmon:
  cakes, 78
  steaks, roasted, with kombu, 74
sandwich(es):
  breads for, 107
  DLTs (dulse, lettuce, and tomato),
    99
  ideas for, 107
  ingredients for, 107
sauce, soy, about, 21
sea lettuce:
  about, 28–29
  condiment, sweetened, 115
sea palm:
  about, 29, 39
  age tofu in, 77
  California, with polenta, 35
  chicken salad, with roasted garlic,
    63
  stew, sweet-and-sour, 39
seared shiitakes, 86
sea vegetable:
  Caesar salad, 55
  kimchee, spicy, 113
  tempura, 80
sea vegetables:
  about, 3–5
  beauty secrets of, 123
  cleaning and soaking of, 17–18
  cultivation and harvest of, 11–15
  history of, 9–11
  mail-order sources for, 124–25
  nutritional benefits of, 5–9
  safe use of, 4–5
  shopping for, 15–16
  storage of, 16–17
seed(s):
  pumpkin, dulse sprinkle, 112
  sesame, jungle green salad with, 66

sesame:
  seeds, jungle green salad with,
    66
  wakame sprinkle, 114
shiitakes, seared, 86
shoyu, about, 21
shrimp:
  -lemongrass-rice soup, 46
  mariscal with, 71
side dishes:
  asparagus with wakame, 95
  Brussels sprouts with smoked dulse and
    water chestnuts, 84
  creamy grapestone in coconut milk,
    85
  dulse mashed potatoes, 96
  frijoles refritos (refried beans), 93
  fucus tip crisps, 98
  hijiki snow peas, 89
  lemony spring vegetables, 83
  seared shiitakes, 86
  simply string beans, 92
  stuffed Chinese cabbage, 90
  wakame succotash, 97
slaw, spiced, 54
smoked dulse, see dulse, smoked
snow peas, hijiki, 89
soba salad, 59
sole, nori-wrapped, 69
soups:
  bonito and kombu stock (dashi),
    49
  classic miso, 40
  creamy white bean, 42
  curried sweet potato, 43
  Italian fava bean, 48
  Korean wakame and beef, 50
  lemongrass-shrimp-rice, 46
  Taiwanese fishermen's, 38

soy sauce, about, 21
spiced slaw, 54
spread, horseradish, for DLTs, 99
spring vegetables, lemony, 83
stews:
    chicken noodle, 45
    sweet-and-sour sea palm, 39
stir-fry, sweet-and-sour tofu, 70
string beans, simply, 92
stroganoff, chicken, 73
stuffed:
    arame-, eggplants, 31
    Chinese cabbage, 90
succotash, wakame, 97
suribachi, 112
sweet-and-sour:
    sea palm stew, 39
    tofu stir-fry, 70
sweet potato soup, curried, 43
sweets and treats:
    apple cider gel, 122
    crispy rice treats, 116
    hazelnut mousse, 117
    three-berry kanten, 119
    trail mix, 120

T

Taiwanese fishermen's soup, 38
tamari, about, 21
tempeh, deep-fried, hijiki with, 82
tempura, sea vegetable, 80
three-berry kanten, 119
tofu:
    age, in sea palm, 77

sweet-and-sour stir-fry,
    70
trail mix, 120

U

umeboshi vinegar, about, 56

V

vegetables:
    lemony spring, 83
    sea, *see* sea vegetables
vinegar:
    brown rice, about, 51
    umeboshi, about, 56

W

wakame:
    about, 30, 43, 95
    asparagus with, 95
    and beef soup, Korean, 50
    sesame sprinkle, 114
    succotash, 97
walnuts, roasted, citrus hijiki with,
    64
water chestnuts, Brussels sprouts with
    smoked dulse and, 84
wild nori in black-eyed peas, 56
wraps:
    brunch burrito, 101
    crispy crepes with nori flakes, 104